Community Forestry

Local Values, Conflict and Forest Governance

Providing a critical and incisive examination of community forestry, this is a detailed study of complex issues in local forest governance, community sustainability, and grassroots environmentalism. It explores community forestry as an alternative form of local collaborative governance in globally significant developed forest regions, with examples ranging from the Gulf Islands of British Columbia to Scandinavia.

Responding to the global trend in devolution of control over forest resources and the ever-increasing need for more sustainable approaches to forest governance, this book highlights both the possibilities and the challenges associated with community forestry. It features compelling case studies and accounts from those directly involved with community forestry efforts, providing unique insight into the underlying social processes, issues, events, and perceptions. It will equip students, researchers, and practitioners with a deep understanding of both the evolution and the management of community forestry in a pan-national context.

RYAN C. L. BULLOCK is a Postdoctoral Fellow in the School of Environment and Sustainability, University of Saskatchewan, Canada. His research addresses environmental governance and conflict in northern and rural settings, and he has served on the Executive Committee of the Canadian Association of Geographers.

KEVIN S. HANNA is an Associate Professor in the Department of Geography and Environmental Studies, Wilfrid Laurier University, Canada. His research centers on integrated approaches to natural resource management, forest sector policy in Canada, environmental impact assessment (EIA), and regional land-use planning.

Community Forestry

Local Values, Conflict and Forest Governance

RYAN C. L. BULLOCK
University of Saskatchewan,
Saskatchewan, Canada

KEVIN S. HANNA
Wilfrid Laurier University,
Ontario, Canada

CAMBRIDGE
UNIVERSITY PRESS

CAMBRIDGE UNIVERSITY PRESS
Cambridge, New York, Melbourne, Madrid, Cape Town,
Singapore, São Paulo, Delhi, Mexico City

Cambridge University Press
The Edinburgh Building, Cambridge CB2 8RU, UK

Published in the United States of America by
Cambridge University Press, New York

www.cambridge.org
Information on this title: www.cambridge.org/9780521190435

© R.C.L. Bullock and K.S. Hanna 2012

First published 2012

Printed in the United Kingdom at the University Press, Cambridge

A catalog record for this publication is available from the British Library

Library of Congress Cataloging in Publication Data

Bullock, Ryan C. L.
Community forestry : local values, conflict and forest governance /
Ryan C. L. Bullock, Kevin S. Hanna.
     p.   cm.
   Includes index.
   ISBN 978-0-521-19043-5 (Hardback) – ISBN 978-0-521-13758-4 (Paperback)
     1. Community forestry.   2. Community forestry–Political aspects.
3. Forest management–Political aspects.   4. Sustainable forestry.   I. Hanna,
Kevin S. (Kevin Stuart), 1961–   II. Title.
   SD561.B85 2012
   333.75–dc23
                                                              2011053359

ISBN 978-0-521-19043-5 Hardback
ISBN 978-0-521-13758-4 Paperback

Contents

Acknowledgements

Ryan Bullock acknowledges the significant contributions of the many people from various forest communities, governments and non-government organizations who shared their insights and energy to make this research and book possible. Their commitment to their own communities and local forests, and their willingness to speak candidly about community forestry issues are especially appreciated. Rich Gerard (Freedom), Don Johnson (Conway), Wendy Scribner (University of New Hampshire Cooperative Extension) and Jim Smith (Creston) deserve recognition for their support. The Northern Ontario Sustainable Communities Partnership and British Columbia Community Forest Association are recognized for providing important learning forums to discuss community forestry ideas and experiences. The Bullock, Farrow, Ryan and Highley families deserve special recognition for their ongoing support, both on the road and at home.

Kevin Hanna thanks Ismo Pölönen, Kaisa Raitio and Minna Pappila for their insights on Scandinavian forestry issues and assistance with Finnish language interpretation.

The research and writing of this book was supported by the Social Sciences and Humanities Research Council (SSHRC) of Canada.

1

Defining concepts and spaces for the re-emergence of community forestry

INTRODUCTION

There is no shortage of places in the world where forests and their resources are subject to acrimonious, even fierce, conflicts. Across a range of jurisdictions, *community forestry* is one of the solutions being promoted. Definitions of community forestry contain the common perspective that local control of local natural resources helps to produce multiple benefits for local communities. Ideally, community forestry is different from conventional forest management and planning approaches. Community-based environmental resource management and planning seeks to achieve sustainability, fairness, and efficiency in relation to tenure arrangements, stakeholder representation, and the use of all available forms of knowledge in decision-making to support ecologically sustainable practice and mitigate conflict. In some instances, the potential for success of community forestry has been diminished by excessive expectations. However, defining a role for communities in managing local forests is a challenge for government agencies, forestry professionals, firms and communities themselves. The approach holds promise, but there are a range of dynamic factors and contextual conditions that influence the impact and efficacy of community forestry. This book provides a critical look at community forestry in North America and Northern Europe, one that seeks a more incisive look at the concept, its promise and its limitations.

COMMUNITIES AND FORESTS

Community forestry is neither a new concept nor a new practice. It represents a traditional and longstanding approach to managing human interactions with forest lands and resources, common in developing regions and among the indigenous societies of developed regions (Poffenberger 1990; Mallik and Rahman 1994; Baker and Kusel 2003; Menzies 2004). Over about the past 150 years, there has been a slow and sporadic adoption of community forestry in North America, typically as an alternative to large-scale industrial and state-run forest management. While community interests often have had to compete with industrial interests and conventional forms of western forestry, a blend of industrial and ecoforestry methods is used in community forests in developed countries (Duinker and Pulkki 1998; Beckley 1998; Krogman and Beckley 2002; Teitelbaum et al. 2006; Bullock et al. 2009). Evidently discord among conventional industrial and community-based approaches has more to do with contrasting principles and vested interests than with actual preferences for forestry practices.

Despite resistance from conventional established interests, there has been a resurgence of community forestry in developing countries since about the 1970s, and even more recent revival in Canada and the United States during the 1990s (Mallik and Rahman 1994; Brendler and Carey 1998). This growth is part of a global trend towards increased local control over natural resources and benefits through community-based natural resource management (CBNRM) (Armitage 2005) and signals a global movement in forest governance reform. A growing body of multidisciplinary evidence now questions the sustainability of conventional forest management (and conventional environmental resource management practice and research in general) based on top-down decision-making, technical and market-based solutions, and sustained yield policies and science (e.g. Behan 1990; Ostrom 1990; Holling 1995; Hutchings et al. 1997; Clapp 1998; Bryant and Wilson 1998; Röling 2002). To address the ecological, economic and social limitations of conventional forest management, there is increased societal demand for more collaborative and adaptive approaches to better include multiple knowledge forms and local and non-state actors with different interests and values, as well as consideration for unique local contextual factors. Such arrangements diverge from the conventional government and industry control over forests, into the realm of forest governance – conceptualized here as the broader involvement of political actors, processes and structures that organize decisions and actions affecting forest regions and societies (see Lemos and Agrawal 2006).

Framed as a more sustainable option to industrial, centralized and top-down forest management, community forestry seems to present a "win–win" situation that can satisfy numerous needs and values. In principle, community forestry is more collaborative and participatory as it frequently involves multi-stakeholder arrangements and seeks to incorporate multiple timber and non-timber values, as well as different, indeed competing, worldviews and knowledge, into human decisions and actions affecting forest ecosystems. Community forestry is also considered as a way to mitigate conflict over resources and territories, empower communities, implement ecologically-based forestry and environmental stewardship, and restore community and cultural links with local environs (Brendler and Carey 1998; Baker and Kusel 2003; Teitelbaum *et al.* 2006; Bullock *et al.* 2009). But community forestry cannot be everything to everybody. Definitions and expectations will vary, and these desires themselves can become the root of new conflicts as community groups deliberate what form and purpose the "new" governance structures should take. There is growing recognition among community forestry practitioners and researchers that the hopeful idealism that at times surrounds the concept must give way to more systematic examinations of actual experiences and lessons learned in various institutional and physical settings (Beckley 1998; Gunter 2004; Bullock and Hanna 2008; Donoghue and Sturtevant 2008). Implementing community forestry in policy and practice is complex and difficult work.

COMMUNITY FORESTRY, COMMUNITY FORESTS AND COMMUNITY-BASED FORESTRY

Community forestry has been widely interpreted by different people in different contexts. Local involvement in environmental resource management, and forest management and planning in particular, falls under many aliases, such as community forestry (Krogman and Beckley 2002; Belsky 2008; Flint *et al.* 2008); community, town or municipal forests (McCullough 1995); indigenous and Aboriginal forestry (Parsons and Prest 2003); community-based natural resource management (Armitage 2005); community-based conservation (Berkes 2003); and co-management (Armitage *et al.* 2007). In general, these terms are used to describe certain institutional conditions that facilitate greater local control over and responsibility for decisions affecting the use of nearby forests, and how and where various forest-derived benefits are distributed. More specifically, the main goals of community forestry are as follows:

1. To enhance local control over decisions affecting forests deemed by communities to hold unique local significance for economic, social and ecological reasons (Belsky 2008; Bullock

Figure 1.1 Community forestry advocates host a public workshop at Lakehead University in northern Ontario, Canada, to create space for public deliberation on the need to reform the provincial forest tenure system (photo R. Bullock).

et al. 2009). Typically, community forestry is implemented to produce more democratic and participatory decision-making processes that include citizens more directly than was previously done under industrial forestry regimes. Community forestry also seeks to improve the diversity, quality and quantity of forest-derived benefits that are generated and their distribution, as opposed to the usual primary sector jobs and revenue streams through timber harvesting and export. While full and direct participation by all residents in decision-making is often considered the ideal (e.g. in a cooperative structure), many communities pursue the desire for better representation and equity through elected shareholder boards that include a range of local stakeholders thought to represent different local values and interests of social groups within the community or region (e.g. conservation groups, indigenous peoples, local government, cottagers, recreationalists, local business and forest industry). Land ownership and tenure are important issues to consider in the local control debate (Figure 1.1). However, advocates see several possible spaces where community forestry could enable local control and benefits ranging from fee simple ownership of private forest land by a community, licensed tenure over state-owned public lands, or partnerships and mixed ownership models that create a variety of arrangements (M'Gonigle 1996; Duinker and Pulkki 1998; Anderson and Horter 2002; Krogman and Beckley 2002; Teitelbaum *et al.* 2006; Belsky 2008). Direct and substantial local control is, however, considered essential.

2. To enhance local economic stability through forest-based economic development (McCullough 1995; Gunter and Jodway 1999). Community forestry is frequently pursued to create formal employment through forestry operations and tourism, and/or enhance opportunities for harvesting timber and non-timber forest products (such as for food and fuel) to supplement residents' livelihoods. There is usually

(a)

Figure 1.2 Contrasting examples of forest-based local economic development. (a) Local economic diversification through wood value-added processing and tourism promotion in Wawa, Ontario, Canada. Former forest worker turned artist and studio owner, Spike Mills, converted his passion for wood carving into a full-time occupation in 2007 when Weyerhaeuser closed its nearby oriented strained board facility, dropping 132 full-time jobs. Though surrounded by northern Ontario's vast public forests, most Crown wood is licensed to major companies (albeit non-operating) and there is no community forest in Wawa. Instead, Mills purchases timbers for his "Faces of Gitchee Goomee" from a private woodlot owner.

(b)

Figure 1.2 (cont.) (b) A two-person crew harvests cord wood destined for local use and export to Quebec. Freedom Town Forest, New Hampshire, USA (photos: R. Bullock).

an emphasis on maintaining a working forest that can promote local employment and local use, and on diversifying local economy through investment in value-added processing (Krogman and Beckley 2002; Teitelbaum *et al.* 2006; Belsky 2008) (Figure 1.2a and b). At its root, community forestry is linked with local economic development and the recirculation of resource and benefit flows within communities, or groups of communities within a region, to improve forest community self-reliance and sustainability. A commitment to the local contrasts greatly with hinterland models that historically have seen most benefits from resource development flow to core and urban regions, both domestically and abroad, while locals are left with the consequences of forest and capital extraction. According to M'Gonigle (1997: 39) moving away from a conventional "centralist" to a new "territorial" model of community forest development would emphasize economic value rather than volume, modes of production that are labor-rather than capital-intensive, and transition from corporate bureaucracies to local decision-making structures.

Figure 1.3 An example of ecosystem-based forest management by a community forest in Creston, British Columbia, Canada. The Creston Valley Forest Corporation uses selective harvesting techniques in its mountainous operating area (background) primarily to protect water quality and quantity for domestic and agricultural consumption (foreground) that supports a lucrative orchard, brewing and tourism industry. Such techniques can preserve viewscapes and aesthetics (pictured here) as well as generating timber revenues and maintaining caribou habitat in the high country (photo: R. Bullock).

3. To enhance sustainable forest management through improved stewardship and ecologically sensitive forestry practices that respect multiple timber and non-timber values (such as timber, water, soil, air and wildlife) and protect cultural, recreational and aesthetic values (Figure 1.3). Internationally, research aimed at evaluating the success of community forestry has tended to focus heavily on ecological sustainability as a key measure (e.g. a community forest's ability to improve actual forest conditions and address degradation) (Padgee *et al.* 2006). In developed regions, the erosion of ecological services, and increasing privatization and subdivision of open spaces into ever-smaller plots (parcelization) threaten local access to forests and forest-derived benefits. Many community forests emerge as residents, landowners, community-based

conservation organizations and indigenous communities respond to local environmental degradation, and related social conflict, caused by industrial forestry operations on both public and private lands (Baker and Kusel 2003; Belsky 2008; Bullock *et al.* 2009). In locales where ecosystem protection and conservation are high priorities, ecoforestry and ecosystem-based management and planning are often attractive for community forest groups, as these approaches offer more ecologically sensitive options, integrate multiple values, and have been endorsed by both indigenous and non-indigenous peoples (Hammond 1991; Slocombe 1993; M'Gonigle 1996; Silva Forest Foundation 2003).

Scholars distinguish between *community forests*, *community forestry* and *community-based forestry*, though the terms are frequently used interchangeably in broad reference to some form of local involvement in forestry decision-making and practice (Krogman and Beckley 2002). In the broadest of interpretations, forestry cooperatives, planning processes with unusually high public participation and research-oriented bridging organizations such model forests are also equated with and researched as community forestry. Semantic differences are often based on varying levels of and distribution of control and benefits, ownership and access, and on the actors involved, as well as whether development and/or conservation values are pursued. However, in developed regions the terms community forest and community forestry are usually reserved for situations where a certain forest land base is collectively owned and managed by its governing political or administrative entity (Belsky 2008; Danks 2008). For Krogman and Beckley (2002: 112) a *community forest* specifically refers to "an entity that has an explicit mandate and legal decision-making authority to manage a given land base for the benefit of a local community," creating a high level of institutionalized community control and benefit. As seen in Chapters 3 through 7 of this volume, community forests in Canada and the United States can include forests owned and managed by a municipality, conservation authority, conservation commission, indigenous community or non-government organization.

While the term *community forestry* also "implies ownership or some type of tenurial arrangement related to [a particular parcel of] forestland" (Danks 2008: 186), others assert that community forestry could be achieved without actual community ownership under conditions where communities and forest managers form a partnership to enhance local benefits relative to previous levels (Krogman and Beckley 2002). Others further classify sub-categories of community forestry according to underlying motivations and contexts. Community forestry serves multiple purposes: as *social forestry* to address deforestation in developing regions; as *small-scale industrial management* aimed at generating economic profit; and as *ecological forestry* which emerges as a response to environmental degradation caused by conventional industrial forestry operations from "outside" the community (McIlveen and Bradshaw 2009). Community forestry is very much about constructing "political space" (St Martin 2001; Pinkerton *et al.* 2008) that is oriented toward local control over resources, distribution of benefits, and decision-making.

Community-based forestry is a still broader concept that, while definitely aligned with the principles behind community forests and community forestry, takes an additional step back to include various potential stakeholders and institutional arrangements. Community-based forestry basically connotes heightened local control and local benefits, as well as local knowledge and technical inputs, and can include small private holdings such as family forests and farms, local government owned forests, and/or situations in which communities and/or non-government organizations share in decision-making and benefits through co-managing public forests with senior governments (Danks 2008). According to Belsky (2008: 219) community-based forestry "usually involves communities and their allies collaboratively interacting to increase their involvement in sustainable public forest land management."

To further complicate matters, *urban forestry* is sometimes equated with community forestry. For example, Gerhold (2007: 2) uses the terms *community forest*, *city green* and *urban forest* interchangeably with reference to the management of "trees, lower vegetation, open grass spaces, and associated wildlife within a municipality or adjacent to it." Lawrence *et al.* (2009) note that in the United Kingdom, community forestry has a strong urban foundation linked to city revival. However, McCullough (1995: 199) distinguishes urban community forestry whose "proponents emphasize care for trees and woodland parks that shade city streets or furnish open spaces" and where the production of wood products "is at best only an incidental part of this program." M'Gonigle (1998) argues that at best such municipal programs represent very limited forms of community forestry, where local representatives have a low level of control over meager forests and are relegated to tree planting. However, the proper management of urban forests does contribute to soil and water improvement, to shade and ground cover, to aesthetics and to recreation, and can include mechanisms for public involvement – all of which are values that are in keeping with traditional community forests and forestry as outlined in the above sections. Urban community forestry comes from a tradition of urban planning and landscape design where managerialism and technocracy still prevail, rather than grassroots natural resource development and stewardship intended to promote community economic and social development (see Kuser 2007). Although nuanced, urban community forestry refers more to the technical approaches for managing trees in the green belts of built environs, whereas present-day community forestry is more closely related to grassroots movements for civic environmentalism and improving local social equity and wellbeing (Baker and Kusel 2003: 5–6).

With all of this in mind, in our book we use the term *community forest* to refer to the land base and associated entity responsible for management decisions. As *community forestry* implies human–forest interactions and the purposeful manipulation of local forests for local human and environmental benefit – that is, what people "do" when involved with community forests – we use community forestry to refer to the broader governance initiatives, institutions, economic relationships and environmental resource management practices that shape, and are shaped by, community interactions with forest ecosystems.

COMMUNITY(IES)

An additional challenge for conceptualizing and implementing community forestry is the inconsistent definition and application of the core concept *community* (Beckley 1998; Flint *et al.* 2008; Harrington *et al.* 2008). While community forestry research now acknowledges the futility and danger of broad-brush analyses and generalizations across local contexts, there is still a need for clear understanding to avoid the ambiguity that often surrounds the concept of community, and to avoid romanticism and indiscriminate usage. Indeed, using the "community" or "local" label to promote environmental resource management and conservation initiatives is impactful. Much like "sustainability," the "community" or "local" label has an inclusive and comforting ring. If you are interested in community, you must be interested in "doing the right thing," making the term perfect for use by various private, public and civic organizations when they want to persuade the public.

By the late 1980s, local grassroots involvement had become a central pillar of environmental resource management and conservation practice and research, and of international aid agency reports. As M'Gonigle (1998) points out, whether in a policy think tank in Washington DC or a First Nations' forum in northern British Columbia, one of the most potent new buzzwords in public policy today is "community." The word also evokes warm feelings associated with grassroots efforts and participation; however, misuse of such terms complicates communication among researchers, weakens research design, and worse, undermines the legitimacy and relevance of communities with respect to forest governance (Flint *et al.* 2008; Sturtevant and Donoghue 2008).

Part of the challenge is that research focussed on developing regions over the last half of the past century created a romantic view of more isolated indigenous communities as smaller, homogeneous, close-knit groups of like-minded people (Agrawal and Gibson 1999; Borgerhoff *et al.* 2005). Puzzled by why some community-based efforts at natural resource management and conservation were more successful than others, political ecologists began to critically assess the notion of community, revealing instead much internal and contextual diversity across settlements. Slowly the realization has emerged that communities do not always exist as tight-knit groups of people with similar history and values, living in a distinct area. A quite different view has evolved, one that sees communities as inevitably diverse in terms of their spatial extent, level of resource dependence and behaviors, leading to the development of unique institutions and variable management outcomes. Indeed, notions of the "mythic community," that is, community as "small, integrated groups using locally evolved norms to manage resources sustainably and equitably . . . capture the realities of few, if any, existing communities" (Agrawal and Gibson 1999: 640).

A variable scale of analysis can reveal divisions within communities that constitute sub-communities or factions that hold different values and interests (Leach *et al.* 1999). And there is greater acceptance that historical, social, political and physical contexts condition the outcomes of community-based management efforts. For example, Plummer and FitzGibbon (2004) call attention to the preconditions, characteristics and related underlying processes that create variation among community-based institutional arrangements and outcomes across different contexts. A prime example of this variation in developed regions is observable among Ontario's 36 conservation authorities, all of which share the same legislated mandate but vary in terms of capacity, stakeholder interests, pro-gramming and operations, and context (Mitchell and Shrubsole 1992; Bullock and Watelet 2006).

The concept of "community" has been widely criticized and is not useful as a generic concept to help identify various groups or *communities* that exist in a given place (e.g. Agrawal and Gibson 1999; Leach *et al.* 1999; Watts 2000; Angeles and Gurstein 2007). For these reasons, some suggest it is more useful to think of a community as having many communities, publics or civil societies (Lee *et al.* 1990; Beckley 1998; Angeles and Gurstein 2007). In forest management these groups are often represented by stakeholders – those individuals or groups considered to hold an interest or stake in decision and outcome effects. This can include parties with legal authority and responsibility for decisions and the associated outcomes (Mitchell 2002).

With respect to community forestry and forest communities, three major types or definitions of community are common. Community forestry researchers and practitioners most commonly use the term *community* to refer to a discrete physical landscape entity and the people living there, variously referred to as *geographical, territorial* or *place-based communities* (Beckley 1998; Teitelbaum *et al.* 2006). A familiarity with place and specific place-related issues is often a unifying factor for "broad-based coalitions of the 'unlike'" (e.g. residents, municipal officials, industry, environmentalists and others) to engage in community-based initiatives (Weber and Herzog 2003). Some imaginative or ecologically grounded place-based communities organize themselves around ecological boundaries rather than strict political-administrative boundaries (Weber and Herzog 2003). Conversely, policy makers and researchers undertaking community assessments to examine a suite of issues in forest communities typically employ political-administrative boundaries to delimit communities for study (Patriquin *et al.* 2007; Sturtevant and Donoghue 2008). Either way, geographically discrete community boundaries can create an "inside–outside binary" that can limit participation in environmental resource management by actually dividing people and places (Harrington *et al.* 2008: 204). This is a significant challenge for forest communities surrounded by public land, given the range of local and national interests and values involved.

Communities of interest contain people who can share a common identity based on links to activities or issues (e.g. forest development or conservation), but these communities transcend geographical ties to a certain place and place-based experiences (Lee *et al.* 1990; Sturtevant and Donoghue 2008). The term community is also used to refer to the *socio-economic system* and patterns of interactions of people in a particular place or geographical area, where analysts are concerned with social behaviors rather than the physical context, or the perceptions and meanings that a group of people may associate with the place (Lee *et al.* 1990).

Analyzing the relationships among functional, territorial and other communities – community as social–ecological system – is the concern of an emerging body of research on forest community resilience (Magis 2010). For M'Gonigle (1998), including the whole community means linking people and the environment as well as future generations, that is to say, the linking of people and place through time. This ecosystem-based conceptualization extends the notion of community beyond human members living on the land:

> when fully defined, the maintenance of such community is the most encompassing foundation of sustainability. It embraces complete continuity with both the spatial (including human and non-human elements) and the temporal dimension; including past, present and future generations. (M'Gonigle 1998: 112)

Likewise, Nozick (1999) seeks an integrated view of community as important to understanding sustainability:

> communities are able to sustain themselves over generations not just on the basis of material wealth or power but also on the basis of something deeper and more intangible – a common identity, purpose and culture that bind people together . . . Its lifeblood is its culture – the ways in which people do things together, local traditions, a geographic landscape, shared experiences of the past, and peoples' dreams and hopes for the future. (Nozick 1999: 19)

Perfect unification of all three sorts of communities (and indeed there are others) rarely occurs in forest settings (or elsewhere for that matter); instead, there is diversity within and across community contexts (Lee *et al.* 1990). It is the intermingling of these different communities in forest settings – the interests, values, perceptions, histories and territorial relationships – that produces the conflict and challenges that community forestry seeks to address, and the community forestry cases and experiences examined as the focus of this book.

CAVEATS

There are several common assumptions and cautions associated with community forestry and community-based natural resource management more broadly, which need to be unpacked in order to critically examine the community forestry concept, its promise and its current challenges. Even advocates of community forestry remind us to be careful not to romanticize the concept or generalize across diverse local contexts (e.g. Duinker and Pulkki 1998; Bullock and Hanna 2008). Below, we consider one primary and three related assumptions important to the emergence of community forestry in developed regions.

The overarching belief is that *community control and management will lead to "better" or more sustainable management of forests and ecosystem services*. The idea that local involvement will automatically induce positive change is a dangerous one. In the first instance it cannot be assumed that all communities are ready and willing to assume control over local resources (Duinker *et al.* 1991; Kellert *et al.* 2000; Berkes 2003). As the following chapters show, the motivations and capacity to manage forests locally are influenced by internal and external factors, and local contexts vary greatly. While there are definitely benefits to the approach in certain settings, community forestry is not as simple to implement as it may seem (Gunter 2004). Community management adds complexity. It is more difficult to deliver than state management programs because of the mix of goals, interests and organizational features produced through devolution and decentralization (Kellert *et al.* 2000).

Given the diversity across community forest cases, the number of factors, feedbacks and cause-and-effect relationships change as management regimes branch outward to make local governance possible. Implementing community forestry comes with different sets of problems that need to be identified and resolved locally in order to make the most of what the approach has to offer (implementation challenges and the dynamics of conflict in local forest governance are reviewed more thoroughly in Chapter 2). The belief that local control will produce better results than conventional approaches rests on at least three related assumptions that tie to the main principles outlined above.

The first is that local people (presumably residents themselves in their lay roles) can and will manage ecosystems in a manner that is widely considered to be more ecologically sound. Much of this rests on the assumption that because people depend on local environmental resources and know the local conditions better than anyone else, and they have to live with the results of management decisions, they will do a great job (Mallik and Rahman 1994; Gunter and Jodway 1999; Flint *et al.* 2008). Indeed, there is growing recognition that knowledge and capacity do exist locally (Wismer and Mitchell 2005). There is much utility in local knowledge and Traditional Ecological Knowledge (TEK), and increasing recognition for the central role of "good" information for managing forests as well as the potential benefits of integration of different types of information (Reed and McIlveen 2006). In particular, TEK, if incorporated in a culturally appropriate manner, can offer insights that sustainable forest managers and planners frequently need but cannot access (Stevenson and Webb 2003). It is also widely held that decision-making that is close to the problems will better address and be more responsive to changing local conditions (Mitchell 2002). However, CBNRM advocates caution that community management does not necessarily ensure the effective incorporation of traditional knowledge, realization of ecological goals, or sustainable use of resources (Kellert *et al.* 2000).

There is also no guarantee that selective logging practices, which are generally considered to be more environmentally and socially viable, will be used by community managers (R. Hood, personal communication, May 2011). For example, Ambus (2008) found little difference between the silvicultural systems used by large-scale industrial forest managers and by community forest managers in British Columbia, suggesting that contextual conditions, rather than some pervasive community forestry ideal, influence decision-making. Moreover, communities that hold licenses for forests on public lands must comply with regulatory frameworks that may or may not support local desires (Burda 1998). Empirical case study analysis of emerging community forest organizations in British Columbia found that communities that would have implemented reduced harvests and alternative harvesting techniques through professionally prepared plans for ecosystem-based forest management were actually constrained by existing tenure arrangements (Bullock *et al.* 2009). And there are cases of industrial community forests that may not focus on conservation and stewardship as a priority (Beckley 1998). Capacity limitations, in terms of having the necessary resources, information, trained personnel and staffing, are oft-cited strikes against community organizations that may also affect practice. Even in rare instances where rural communities have produced and possess a strong resource information base and are in a position to integrate local and scientific knowledge for better decision-making and action, these efforts can be hindered by conflicted social relations among groups with varying levels of influence (Peterson 2007).

A second crucial point of caution is in the assumption that devolved decision-making processes are somehow inherently more democratic and will lead to forest management that is more socially sustainable. There is unconditional faith that local decision-making will be more representative and fair in terms of inclusiveness through bottom-up incorporation of a broad range of interests, values and conventionally marginalized groups (e.g. youth, women, indigenous groups). Community-based approaches also promise to enable indigenous involvement in a manner that helps to preserve cultural autonomy (Agrawal and Gibson 1999). However, the equitable redistribution of power and benefits is not automatic but requires carefully designed institutions to balance power relations (Berkes 2003; Colfer 2005). The potential for co-option by local elites can be high. There are cases in which "new" community-based institutions, introduced to support more sustainable and equitable resource decision-making for local forest and resource-based development, have simply recreated existing power relations that favored previously dominant actors (Reed 1995; Bullock 2010). Moreover, forest community initiatives often experience difficulty in responding to shifting internal and external demographics and societal preferences that dictate local lifestyles and economy and put pressure on what can and cannot be done through local decision-making (Gill and Reed 1997; Kruger *et al.* 2008; Bullock *et al.* 2009).

A third caveat relates to the claim that local control and more inclusive access to forest resources will produce economies and communities that are more innovative and economically viable. Research in resource-based communities shows that efforts to implement community-based environmental resource management for economic development can be quite effectively obstructed by local business elites to instead maintain a narrow set of conventional economic values and stakeholders (Reed 1995). However, when they work, "management practices within community forests are generally more innovative, diverse and labor intensive than other forms of tenure and provisions are made for a broader spectrum of forest values" (Haley 2002: 61). It is believed that local control enables the best end use of timber and value-added uses to produce more forest-derived benefits that reach more people (M'Gonigle 1998). It is also possible that community forestry will sustain local economic development activity through time, at least at more constant levels than previously experienced in boom and bust economies, because of a commitment to community (Duinker *et al.* 1991). Some propose that community forestry will mobilize dormant talent in underdeveloped extractive regions. Here, talent has been historically drained off to core regions or left to stagnate under an industrial economic model that seeks merely to produce dimensional timber requiring only basic training and skill development, leaving youth and forest workers little incentive to think creatively about wood, and invest their energy and money in their dreams (Robinson 2009). While convincing and worthwhile pursuits, practical examples of community forestry illustrate that economic viability of the community forest organizations and operations must precede marked economic returns to the host community (as with the Creston Valley Forest Corporation, Chapter 5 in this book). Positive outcomes or benefits must be assessed based on ecological and social metrics as well. Unfortunately, social scientists who advocate community forestry have not had the opportunity to see their theories translated into widespread practice in developed regions, and so have to rest on the supposition that community forestry will produce more wealth *if* we can get the conditions and incentives "just right." While it seems that conventional industrial forestry has failed most forest communities, experience with community forestry shows that wealth generation and distribution is not automatic.

THE ROAD AHEAD

The following chapters address the need for empirical research and dialogue on community forests in order to share the experiences and lessons – both good and bad – and help develop understanding, theory and practice for creating and managing successful community forests. This book focuses on community forestry as an alternative form of forest governance in developed regions, and on the challenges and lessons associated with community forestry implementation and conflict. The stories and observations presented herein are based on research conducted between 2004 and 2010. We employed case study research methods, including site visits, semi-structured interviews, document review and a review of published cases and narratives, to document, analyze and interpret different experiences with community forestry across Canada, the United States and Northern Europe. The voices of those directly involved with community forest efforts are included in the form of previously cited quotations gleaned from historical public documents and academic articles or chapters, or direct anonymous quotations from our interview data, which have been assigned aliases. The result is a collection of illustrative cases that present prominent local and regional events, perceptions and challenges encountered when putting community forestry into practice.

Chapter 1 provides a brief and critical introduction to the challenges of contemporary forest management and the emergence of community forestry as a response, as well as some foundational concepts and arguments that pervade the community forestry literature. Chapter 2 examines the role of community forestry in conflict mitigation, with an emphasis on linking the literature on conflict and implementation to work on forest management and CBNRM. We consider community forestry as a vehicle for integrating diverse values into forest resource management across diverse tenure settings, but show how it may also engender social conflict. Circumstances that aid or inhibit the effective development and implementation of community forestry are also explored. In Chapter 3 we present cases of community forestry in New England and examine how communities have become part of the fabric of forest management in the northeastern United States. Drawing from examples in New Hampshire and Vermont, the role of communities, non-government organizations and local landowners is described and linked to broader concepts in community forestry. The parallel experiences of community forestry in Ontario, Canada are the subject of Chapter 4. A review of community forestry policies and models in Ontario illustrates how the concept has been tested during times of heightened concern for ecological degradation, social conflict and economic disaster, and despite its longstanding successes, remains subject to resistance from entrenched interests that preserve the status quo on public forest lands. In Chapter 5 we describe a pivotal case and the ongoing challenges in what has been widely regarded as a success story for community forestry and watershed management in Canada. The emergence and later operational struggles of the Creston Valley Forest Corporation in British Columbia are discussed with an eye to the implementation challenges experienced during its early phase. Chapter 6 compares the experiences of two island communities to illustrate barriers to implementing community forestry on British Columbia's Pacific coast. In particular, issues pertaining to cross-cultural relations, local politics and the latent growth control agenda in community forestry are discussed. For Chapter 7 we review how community forestry has been interpreted and applied with respect to local involvement and forest governance in the southwestern United States. Reflective and comparative, Chapter 8 juxtaposes concepts and experiences from the North American chapters with forest management and use in northern Europe. We explore a range of tenures that operate within a setting that has emphasized a top-down approach to forest policy, and consider how an engrained culture of forest stewardship and increasing demand for a community voice have created a new dialogue about how local values can be best incorporated into a complex management and tenure setting. Chapter 9 provides a synthesis and discussion of community forestry issues and themes presented in this book.

REFERENCES

Agrawal, A. and Gibson, C. (1999). Enchantment and disenchantment: The role of community in natural resource conservation. *World Development* **27**(4): 629–49.

Ambus, L. (2008). The evolution of devolution: evaluation of the Community Forest Agreement in British Columbia. Unpublished Master's thesis University of British Columbia, Vancouver, Canada.

Anderson, N. and Horter, W. (2002). *Connecting Lands and People: Community Forests in British Columbia*. Victoria: Dogwood Initiative.

Angeles, L. and Gurstein, P. (2007). Learning civil societies for democratic planning and governance. In Gurstein, P. and Angeles, L. (eds.), *Learning Civil Societies: Shifting Contexts for Democratic Planning and Governance*. Toronto: University of Toronto Press, pp. 3–22.

Armitage, D. (2005). Adaptive capacity and community-based natural resource management. *Environmental Management* **35**(6): 703–15.

Armitage, D., Berkes, F. and Doubleday, D. (eds.) (2007). *Adaptive Co-Management: Collaboration, Learning and Multi-Level Governance*. Vancouver, BC: UBC Press.

Baker, M. and Kusel, J. (2003). *Community Forestry in the United States*. Washington, DC: Island Press.

Beckley, T. (1998). Moving toward consensus-based forest management: A comparison of industrial, co-managed, community and small private forests in Canada. *Forestry Chronicle* **74**(5): 736–44.

Behan, R. (1990). Multiresource forest management: A paradigmatic challenge to professional forestry. *Journal of Forestry* **88**(4): 12–18.

Belsky, J. (2008). Creating community forests. In Donoghue, E. and Sturtevant, V. (eds.), *Forest Community Connections. Implications for Research, Management and Governance*. Washington, DC: Resources for the Future, pp. 219–42.

Berkes, F. (2003). Rethinking community-based conservation. *Conservation Biology* **18**(3): 621–30.

Brendler, T. and Carey, H. (1998). Community forestry, defined. *Journal of Forestry* **96**(3): 21–3.

Bryant, R. and Wilson, G. (1998). Rethinking environmental management. *Progress in Human Geography* **22**(3): 321–43.

Bullock, R. (2006). An analysis of community forest implementation in British Columbia, Canada. Unpublished MES thesis. Wilfrid Laurier University, Waterloo, Ontario.

Bullock, R. (2010). A critical frame analysis of Northern Ontario's "forestry crisis". Unpublished PhD dissertation. University of Waterloo, Waterloo, Ontario.

Bullock, R. and Hanna, K. (2008). Community forestry: Mitigating or creating conflict in British Columbia: *Society and Natural Resources* **21**(1): 77–85.

Bullock, R., Hanna, K. and Slocombe, S. (2009). Learning from community forestry experience: Challenges and lessons from British Columbia. *Forestry Chronicle* **85**(2): 293–304.

Bullock, R. and Watelet, A. (2006). Exploring conservation authority operations in Sudbury, Northern Ontario: Constraints and opportunities. *Environments* **34**(2): 29–50.

Burda, C. (1998). Forests in trust: A blueprint for tenure reform and Community Forestry in British Columbia. *Ecoforestry* May: 12–15.

Borgerhoff Mulder, M. and Coppolillo, P. (2005). *Conservation: Linking Ecology, Economics, and Culture*. Princeton, New Jersey: Princeton University Press.

Clapp, R.A. (1998). The resource cycle in forestry and fishing. *Canadian Geographer* **42**(2): 129–44.

Colfer, C. (2005). *The Equitable Forest: Diversity, Community, and Resource Management*. Washington, DC: Resources for the Future.

Danks, C. (2008). Institutional arrangements in community-based forestry. In Donoghue, E. and Sturtevant, V. (eds.) *Forest Community Connections. Implications for Research, Management and Governance*. Washington, DC: Resources for the Future, pp. 185–204.

Donoghue, E. and Sturtevant, V. (eds.) (2008). *Forest Community Connections. Implications for Research, Management and Governance*. Washington, DC: Resources for the Future.

Duinker, P., Matakala, P. and Zhang, D. (1991). Community forestry and its implications for Northern Ontario. *Forestry Chronicle* **67**(2): 131–5.

Duinker, P. and Pulkki, R. (1998). Community forestry, Italian style: The Magnifica Comunita di Fiemme. *Forestry Chronicle* **74**: 385–92.

Flint, C., Luloff, A. and Finley, J. (2008). Where is "community" in community-based forestry? *Society and Natural Resources* **21**: 526–37.

Gerhold, H. (2007). Origins of urban forestry. In Kuser, J. (ed.), *Urban and Community Forestry in the Northeast*, second edition. New York: Springer, pp. 1–24.

Gill, A. and Reed, M. (1997). The reimaging of a Canadian resource town: Post-productivism in a North American context. *Applied Geographic Studies* **1**(2): 129–47.

Gunter, J. (ed.) (2004). *The Community Forest Guidebook: Tools and Techniques for Communities in British Columbia*. Kamloops and Kaslo: Forest Research Extension Partnership and British Columbia Community Forest Association, No. 15.

Gunter, J. and Jodway, S. (1999). Community-based natural resource management: A strategy for community economic development. *CED for Forest Communities Project (draft paper)*. Simon Fraser University, British Columbia.

Haley, D. (2002). Community forests in British Columbia: The past is prologue. *Forest, Trees, and People* **46**: 54–61.

Hammond, H. (1991). *Seeing the Forest among the Trees: The Case for Wholistic Forest Use*. Vancouver, BC: Polestar Press Ltd.

Harrington, C., Curtis, A. and Black, R. (2008). Locating communities in natural resource management. *Journal of Environmental Policy and Planning* **10**(2): 199–215.

Holling, C.S. (1995). What barriers? What bridges? In Gunderson, L., Holling, C.S. and Light, S. (eds.), *Barriers and Bridges to the Renewal of Ecosystems and Institutions*. New York: Columbia University Press, pp. 3–36.

Hutchings, J., Walters, C. and Haedrich, R. (1997). Is scientific inquiry incompatible with government information control? *Canadian Journal of Fisheries and Aquatic Sciences* **54**: 1198–210.

Kellert, S., Mehta, J., Ebbin, S. and Lichtenfeld, L. (2000). Community natural resource management: Promise, rhetoric, and reality. *Society and Natural Resources* **13**: 705–15.

Kruger, L., Mazza, R. and Stielef, M. (2008). Amenity migration, rural communities, and public lands. In Donoghue, E. and Sturtevant, V. (eds.) *Forest*

Community Connections. Implications for Research, Management and Governance. Washington, DC: Resources for the Future, pp. 127–42.

Krogman, N. and Beckley, T. (2002). Corporate "bail-outs" and local "buyouts": Pathways to community forestry? *Society and Natural Resources* **15**: 109–27.

Kuser, J. (ed.). (2007). *Urban and Community Forestry in the Northeast*, second edition. New York: Springer.

Lawrence, A., Anglezarke, B., Frost, B., Nolan, P. and Owen, R. (2009). What does community forestry mean in a devolved Great Britain? *International Forestry Review* **11**(2): 281–97.

Leach, M., Mearns, R. and Scoones, I. (1999). Environmental entitlements: Dynamics and institutions in community-based natural resource management. *World Development* **27**(2): 225–47.

Lee, R., Field, D. and Burch, W. (1990). Introduction: Forestry, community, and sociology of natural resources. In Lee, R., Field, D. and Burch, W. (eds.), *Community and Forestry: Continuities in the Sociology of Natural Resources*. Boulder, San Francisco and London: Westview Press, pp. 3–14.

Lemos, M. and Agrawal, A. (2006). Environmental governance. *Annual Review of Environment and Resources* **31**: 297–325.

Magis, K. (2010). Community resilience: An indicator of social sustainability. *Society and Natural Resources* **23**(5): 401–16.

Mallik, A. and Rahman, H. (1994). Community forestry in developed and developing countries: A comparative study. *Forestry Chronicle* **70**(6): 731–35.

McCullough, R. (1995). *Landscape of Community: A History of Communal Forest in New England*. Hanover, New Hampshire: University of New England Press.

McIlveen, K. and Bradshaw, B. (2009). Community forestry in British Columbia, Canada: The role of local community support and participation. *Local Environment* **14**(2): 193–205.

Menzies, N. (2004). Communities and their partners: Governance and community-based forest management. *Conservation and Society* **2**(2): 449–56.

M'Gonigle, M. (1996). *Living Communities in a Living Forest: Towards an Ecosystem-Based Structure of Local Tenure and Management*. Discussion paper. Victoria, BC.

M'Gonigle, M. (1997). Reinventing British Columbia: Towards a new political economy in the forest. In Barnes T. and Hayter, R. (eds.), *Troubles in the Rainforest: British Columbia's Forest Economy in Transition*. Victoria: Western Geographical Press, pp. 37–52.

M'Gonigle, M. (1998). Structural instruments and sustainable forests: A political ecology approach. In Tollefson, C. (ed.), *The Wealth of Forests: Markets, Regulation, and Sustainable Forestry*. Vancouver, BC: UBC Press, pp. 102–20.

Mitchell, B. (2002). *Resource and Environmental Management*. Harlow, England and NewYork: Prentice Hall/Pearson Education.

Mitchell, B. and Shrubsole, D. (1992). *Ontario Conservation Authorities: Myth and Reality*. Waterloo, Ontario: Department of Geography, University of Waterloo.

Nozick, M. (1999). Sustainable development begins at home: Community solutions to global problems. In Pierce J. and Dale, A. (eds.), *Communities, Development, and Sustainability Across Canada*. Vancouver, BC: UBC Press, pp. 3–23.

Ostrom, E. (1990). *Governing the Commons: The Evolution of Institutions for Collective Action*. Cambridge, England; New York: Cambridge University Press.

Padgee, A., Kim, Y. and Daugherty, P. (2006). What makes community forest management successful? A meta-study from community forests throughout the world. *Society and Natural Resources* **19**: 33–52.

Parsons, R. and Prest, G. (2003). Aboriginal forestry in Canada. *Forestry Chronicle* **79**(4): 779–84.

Patriquin, M., Parkins, J. and Stedman, R. (2007). Socio-economic status of boreal communities in Canada. *Forestry: An International Journal of Forest Research*, **80**(3): 279–91.

Peterson, G. (2007). Using scenario planning to enable an adaptive co-management process in the Northern Highlands Lake District of Wisconsin. In Armitage, D., Berkes, F. and Doubleday, D. (eds.). *Adaptive Co-management: Collaboration, Learning and Multi-Level Governance*. Vancouver, BC: UBC Press, pp. 286–307.

Pinkerton, E., Heaslip, R., Silver, J. and Furman, K.. (2008). Finding "space" for comanagement of forests within the neoliberal paradigm: Rights, strategies, and tools for asserting a local agenda. *Human Ecology*, **36**: 343–55.

Plummer, R. and FitzGibbon, J. (2004). Co-management of natural resources: A proposed framework. *Environmental Management* **33**(6): 876–85.

Poffenberger, M. (1990). *Keepers of the Forest: Land Management Alternatives in Southeast Asia*. Hartford, CT: Kumarian Press Library of Management Development.

Reed, M. (1995). Cooperative management of environmental resources: A case-study from Northern Ontario, Canada. *Economic Geography* **71**(2): 132–49.

Reed, M. and McIlveen, K. (2006). Toward a pluralistic civic science? Assessing community forestry. *Society and Natural Resources* **19**: 591–607.

Robinson, D. (2009). Dark horses and tenure reform. *Northern Ontario Business*, June issue. Available at: http://www.northernontariobusiness.com/DisplayArticle.aspx?id=19211&terms=dark%20horses/ Accessed July 1, 2011.

Röling, N. (2002). Beyond the aggregation of individual preferences. In Leeuwis, C. and Pyburn, R. (eds.), *Wheelbarrows Full of Frogs: Social Learning in Rural Resource Management*. Assen, Netherlands, Koninklijke: Van Gorcum, pp. 25–47.

Silva Forest Foundation (2003). *The Power of Community: Ecosystem-based Conservation Planning across Canada*. British Columbia, Canada: Silva Forest Foundation.

Slocombe, S. (1993). Implementing ecosystem-based management: Development of theory, practice, and research for planning and managing a region. *Bioscience* **43**(9): 612–22.

St Martin, K. (2001). Making space for community resource management in fisheries. *Annals of the Association of American Geographers* **91**: 122–42.

Stevenson, M. and Webb, J. (2003). Just another stakeholder? First Nations and sustainable forest management in Canada's boreal forest. In Burton, P., Messier, C., Smith, D. and Adamowicz, A. (eds.), *Towards Sustainable Management of the Boreal Forest*. Ottawa: National Research Press, pp. 65–112.

Sturtevant, E. and Donoghue, V. (2008). Community and forest connections: Continuity and change. In Donoghue, E. and Sturtevant, V. (eds.), *Forest Community Connections. Implications for Research, Management and Governance* Washington, DC: Resources for the Future, pp. 3–26.

Teitelbaum, S., Beckley, T. and Nadeau, S. (2006). A national portrait of community forestry on public land in Canada. *Forestry Chronicle* **82**(3): 416–28.

Watts, M. (2000). Political ecology. In Sheppard, E. and Barnes, T.J. (eds.), *A Companion to Economic Geography*. Maldem, MA; Oxford, UK: Blackwell Publishers, pp. 257–74.

Weber, E. and Herzog, C. (2003). Connecting the dots: United States grass-roots ecosystem management and sustainable communities. In Shindler, B., Beckley, T. and Finley, M. (eds.), *Two Paths Toward Sustainable Forests: Public Values in Canada and the United States*. Corvallis: Oregon State University Press, pp. 170–93.

Wismer, S. and Mitchell, B. (2005). Community-based approaches to resource and environmental management. *Environments* **33**(1): 1–4.

2

Putting community forestry into place: implementation and conflict

If a community decides to create a community forest, what comes next? Even arriving at the community forestry decision can be contentious and difficult, but making it a reality poses a range of challenges. At one time there was an assumption that once a policy decision was made, its execution became a simple and mundane affair that did not merit significant attention (Hyder 1984). When it came to program or policy efficacy, it was the quality of the idea, or the correctness of the ideology which gave birth to ideas, that mattered. Policy implementation followed naturally; it was an ordinary process that would have little impact on the success of the policy concept. It is fair to say that some institutions still approach the policy process under this assumption.

The understanding of governance and modern government has become more experienced, and a substantial body of research on evaluation has emerged and slowly matured. Audit techniques have also progressed away from an obsession with numbers, and now incorporate qualitative tools that seek to assess efficacy and policy impacts and to understand the social–cultural, contextual and institutional factors that affect policy success. While ideas certainly matter, when it comes to putting them into practice even the best can go awry. In the policy process the implementation stage is without doubt integral to the successful application, and in some respects to the very practicability, of ideas.

Implementation can be defined broadly in two basic ways: first, as the stage between decision and action where the underlying issue is whether the decision will, or can, actually be realized in a manner consistent with the policy objective (Brekke 1987; Hessing and Howlett

23

1997); and second, as a continuing activity where the focus is on analyzing the way that policies or programs function (Freeman 1980; Rossi
and Freeman 1985; Brekke 1987). The latter implies the monitoring,
audit and improvement of activities, which may be complete or still in
progress. Implementation is always a dynamic process. Regardless of
the governance setting, it routinely involves negotiation, compromise
and shifting goals (Ham and Hill 1993). Implementation is not just an
administrative event – one that can be evaluated in terms of which
components do or do not perform as expected or might be required;
rather, it is a policy/action continuum in which an interactive and
negotiative process happens over time (Ham and Hill 1993). There are
occasions when the time it takes to put a policy into action can be
frustratingly long. Negotiative elements emerge in particular when
conflict is an inherent part of the process and setting within which
policy is formed and put into place. Since community forestry initiatives often require institutional support and a change in organizational
relationships, adversarial dynamics have to be recognized and dealt
with when a community-based model is developed, accepted and eventually implemented. If the initiative means a change in tenure arrangements, then there will inevitably be stresses on power relationships.

Challenges to policy implementation have been variously
described as "activities common to the [implementation] process" (Jones
1984), "obstacles to be overcome" (Mitchell 2002), "conditions to be met
for implementation success" (Sabatier and Mazmanian 1981), essential
factors that determine policy success (Van Meter and Van Horn 1975), or
factors that shape instrument choice (Linder and Peters 1989). These are
broad notions, but no matter how they are grouped, frequent elements
(or macro-obstacles) are evident. Seven key obstacle realms have
emerged in the implementation literature (cf. Sabatier and Mazmanian
1981; Walther 1987; Baker 1989; Weale 1992; Margerum and Born 1995
and 2000; Margerum 1999; Mitchell 2002), which are relevant to community forestry implementation.

1. *Tractability.* While tractability is an essential issue in policy
   implementation, it runs the risk of being used to avoid making
   changes to tenure or management approaches. Tractability
   implies complexity of the context. It includes factors such as
   the boundary, the extent to which management authority
   would have to be restructured, the extent of institutional
   behavioral change that might be required, and the degree to
   which community forestry can really solve social, economic

and environmental problems and needs. It also suggests "agency," capacity and resource needs, including not only administrative costs but also operational simplicity. In essence, given the institutional, tenure and conflict setting, how will community forestry help manage the problems?

2. *Clarity of objectives.* Clear objectives not only support the communication of an implementation strategy, but also can be used to delineate the responsibilities of stakeholders. Clarity asks that forest managers and the enabling frameworks for community forestry (such as legislation, regulations or agreements) be structured to maximize the probability that target groups understand their obligations within the community forestry context, and ultimately support efficacy (Sabatier and Mazmanian 1981). Clear objectives also aid in audit and evaluation of success (Mitchell 2002). But there can be a tendency to avoid clarity in order to get a community forestry initiative accepted and put into place. This can be manifest in putting off addressing conflicting goals (extraction versus preservation is a good example). Community forestry in a conflictual and complex setting may begin with vague objectives in order to encourage participation by and the support of diverse stakeholders. Deliberate vagueness is also favored by adaptive approaches – it allows for flexibility as the social/economic or environmental dynamics of the setting change. There may be an assumption that expectations will be more clearly articulated as a program develops, as more information about the extent of a problem is collected, or as more resources are allocated. This may seem pragmatic, but it carries risks, such as the very real threat that key social or economic conflicts cannot be resolved later.

3. *Understanding of cause-and-effect relationships.* If policy is to be successful, there must be an understanding of the links between activities and goals (Mitchell 2002). However, beyond involving knowledge of the impact of community forestry on community wellbeing and its ability to sustain an economy, understanding cause-and-effect relationships means knowing how social and economic systems interact, and understanding if economic decline can really be addressed by injecting more community control into forest management. Implementing community forestry requires ensuring that the enabling framework incorporates sound theory, and has the capacity to

identify and address the primary factors and causal links that
will affect the achievability of what is hoped for from
community forestry.

4. *Commitment.* Stakeholder commitment to policy success is an
essential aspect of implementation (Mitchell 2002). But not all
stakeholders are created equal. Commitment by key agencies,
by resource managers or at the political level often determines
success of community forestry, despite the rhetoric of public
consultation and broad stakeholder support that often
accompanies integration. In some respects, this commitment
can be characterized in terms of gaining legitimacy among key
players (Mitchell 1986; Walther 1987; Margerum and Born
1995; Margerum 1999). With legitimacy, meaningful
commitment will likely follow. This is a pervasive challenge in
community forestry. Agencies may mouth commitment, but
they have little interest, or perhaps little latitude, in making
the substantive changes to tenure and decision-making that
would be essential to (meaningful) community forestry
implementation. The challenge of commitment also means
ensuring that the concept of community forestry, however it
gets defined, is supported by those who hold authority, and
that sufficient jurisdiction is granted to those individuals or
governance structures ultimately responsible for
implementation. Commitment is demonstrated not only
through authority but also through the allocation of sufficient
resources.

5. *Knowledge.* Knowledge gaps and uncertainty about the nature
of the problems that community forestry is intended to
address limit the ability of policy actors to identify causal
linkages or the likelihood that a community forestry approach
will achieve the policy objective(s). Information also presents a
paradox. On the one hand, knowledge may be an essential
aspect of community forestry development, especially aiding
local understanding of the temporal and spatial aspects of
forests and resources to be managed; but there are challenges
in collecting, processing and incorporating scientific, local and
traditional knowledge into planning and management
processes. Knowledge development can be a key activity of
community forestry well before a program or plan can be
outlined and decisions made about its specific use
characteristics, authority of management bodies, and even

location. Knowledge development has its own challenges. More "studying the problem" might also be seen as a stalling tactic. Thus, perpetual research can become a way of avoiding doing something, delaying implementation or indeed fuelling conflict as debates over the sources of knowledge emerge.

6. *Conflict history*. Walther (1987), writing about integrated resource management, comments that successful implementation and impact management are largely a function of the historical context into which the program is inserted. The argument holds true for community forestry. Legacies of conflict and cooperation, planning, resources and timing (the stage of the problem at which it is implemented) are dominant elements in implementation success. Walther recognizes other elements, but the historical context, notably with respect to conflict and cooperation legacies, can impose significant implementation challenges.

7. *Power of personalities*. "Community" has at its definitional core the notion of interaction, between individuals, governance structures and places. Agency, business and conservation interests are represented by individuals, who bring their biases, ideologies, personal experiences, likes and dislikes, and fears to any process. Conflict, and in some locales very acrimonious conflict, is a common feature of community forestry setting. In some settings, successful community forestry implementation will depend very much on who is at the table and whether they get along with, listen to, and even like each other. Overcoming entrenched and frequently ardent positions that can characterize land use and management approaches, and notions of who should make decisions, is indeed a difficult task for those involved in community forestry; nevertheless, it seems to be a pivotal expectation that community forestry will provide the means and the setting for bringing together a community.

8. *Unique challenges*. Since each policy setting provides unique challenges, factors that may be unique to the setting, policy or program should also be considered. Mitchell (2002) refers to cultural challenges, notably within the context of the developing world. Rayner (1991) notes the importance of ideological perspectives, not only in implementation but reflected in different concepts of managerialism that stream from political-economic ideology. These may favor certain

approaches to production, management and forest use. Corruption, political influence, incompetence and nepotism may also emerge as issues quite apart from all others. These can be more difficult to identify, let alone prove, and certainly address. However, transparency and openness can go a long way toward alleviating such dynamics.

There can also be a great disconnect between the policy instruments available to implementing agencies and the expectations or culture of affected communities. It may simply be that community forestry, beyond enhancing consultation, cannot be implemented because the institutional setting for providing tenure or making decisions is not suited, and cannot be easily changed. Baker and Kusel (2003: 13) comment that in spite of the long history of ideas and support for community forestry in North America, "the marginalization throughout most of the last century of these traditions and ideas warns us of the power and influences of forces that would prefer to see community forestry fail." In the first instance, establishing the idea in the collective mindset of citizens, forestry practitioners and schools, business people and policy makers remains an important step towards wider acceptance, real support, and ultimately, change. And while a lack of capacity in many small towns, limited bureaucratic imagination, poor political support, and industry dominance are all factors frequently touted to work against implementing community forestry, no single variable really dominates. In our experience, complex interactions among numerous factors and invisible pathways to change stand to thwart even highly organized, energized and politically supported initiatives, and thus make implementation difficult. These may not even be purposeful; rather they emerge as part of the natural tensions that characterize communities and inevitably color the interactions of individuals.

It may also be that in some contexts a form of trap exists, where the need for change is recognized and accepted, but social or economic elements render communities seemingly unable to adapt, change or implement new systems – something that fits with the characterization of a *social trap* (Platt 1973). This can result in a form of community paralysis which may eventually manifest in conflict, and blame when things do not work out or social and economic conditions become worse. Conflict within a forest-based community can be born from a desperation that results from declining opportunities and the often very sudden realization that things are no longer as they once were and a seemingly sustainable industry and way of life can no longer be sustained. Implementation in such settings is, to say the least, difficult, until consensus for the need to change is first realized, and then relative agreement is reached on the source(s) of conflict and what change(s) should look like.

THE CHARACTER OF CONFLICT

While conflict may commonly be a catalyst for moving communities to think about change, conflict may also linger long after a community forestry initiative has been defined and implemented. Conflict should be characterized as broadly as possible in terms of its origins and qualities (Easterbrook *et al.* 1993). Having said this, it also helps to view it as having three general characteristics: interaction (of individuals), interdependence (individuals must interact for some reason) and incompatibility with respect to goals (for whatever reason they do not agree on the goals, aims or objectives, or how to achieve them) (Putnam and Poole 1987). This notion is broad enough to encompass a myriad of nuanced definitions. There is an extensive literature on the causes of conflict, each with particular relevance to specific problem contexts. In examining community forestry we have come to focus on three conditions which seem recurrent, regardless of the setting: *communicative* and *deliberative*, *personal dynamics* and *processual* issues.

Communicative refers to the interactive discursive context, which includes information exchange, development and transfer of knowledge, semantic and language elements, discourse and methods of interaction which may proceed individually or interactively (Dorcey 1986; Robbins 1989; Forester 1999). The ingredients of this "context" ultimately affect understanding and construct relationships. Personal dynamics include values, or ideas held, and beliefs (interpretation of information or understanding of cognitive substance), preferences and tastes, interests and ideology, and even personalities (Deutsch 1973; Robbins 1989). The success of group interaction in resource and environmental management often hinges on personal elements and in particular the history of their relations. On the other hand, processual and deliberative factors describe the institutional arrangements (administrative and governance settings) for community deliberation, capacity to act, and the all-encompassing notion of power – specifically who has it and how they tend to use it (Putnam and Poole 1987; Robbins 1989; Briggs 1998; Forester 1999). These are issues that are ubiquitous in community forestry.

Individual causes of conflict are not mutually exclusive; rather, it is most common that different types of conflict will emerge and occur simultaneously (Mitchell 2002). Nor should conflict always be seen as a negative force. Conflict simply says that a problem exists; it can indicate process weakness, reveal aspects of a decision that need to be reconsidered, or be the catalyst for bringing new information, knowledge and community values to the fore. Innovation and creativity are often products of conflict, and it can force agencies away from the status quo and into a realm of policy and operational innovation and community consultation. If community forestry is an innovation in forest management, then its conflict origins would seem to support this assertion. On the other hand, conflict can build barriers between groups, fracture processes or weaken implementation. If left unresolved, conflict can disintegrate relationships and create misinformation, misunderstanding, bias and a lack of trust (Johnson and Duinker 1993). That is quite apparent in some of the cases we describe in this book.

CONFLICT AS A DYNAMIC ELEMENT IN COMMUNITY FOREST GOVERNANCE

Communicative

Perhaps the strongest attribute of the community forest model is the opportunity it provides for reducing cognitive conflicts between different parties. The arrangement of local interests into a multi-stakeholder situation increases opportunities for direct and frequent interaction among participants, where the chance to gather and share information in its many forms among the different sources is a key strength – as information sharing advances, mutual understanding and trust may follow. However, this exchange depends heavily on effective communication and open-mindedness among participants, which can be hampered by behavioral conflicts.

Under more conventional management schemes, local input has been limited by the "science knows best" approach of forestry professionals in industry and government. This might be described as a participation-limited model, where interaction is between managers and scientist with little external input (Kusel *et al.* 1996). Robinson *et al.* (2001: 29) see the sometimes "indifference" of forest managers with respect to consultation as emanating from a frustration over public ignorance of forest issues. Certainly there is orthodoxy in professional forestry, based in the utilitarian tenets of scientific forestry and focused on "the science of timber extraction and regeneration for maximizing financial returns through timber values" (Beckley 1998: 741). This belief has not only been quite effectively maintained in the entwined relationship between government and industry, but also within academic forestry and professional forestry bodies. In an "elitist," indeed parochial setting, it is hardly surprising that the merits of other forms of knowledge have often been discounted by forestry institutions, but this is changing.

One of the expectations of a community forestry approach is that it serves as an enabling mechanism for non-traditional sources and forms of knowledge in forest management. Typically this means traditional knowledge (experiential, estimative and predictive) and information (observational and factual) from Aboriginal people, hunters and anglers, naturalists, loggers and back country users and environmentalists to name a few who inevitably possess first-hand knowledge of regional and some-times vast landscapes and of the shifting conditions that reflect environ-mental change, whether natural or human induced. The "public" offers "valuable lay knowledge and subjective perceptions" that improve the overall information base (Allan and Frank 1994). It is just for that reason

> natural resource managers stand to gain considerable insight, information and knowledge from community members, including indigenous and local knowledge, detailed understanding of the on-the-ground social and economic impacts of agency policies and procedures and the synergistic effects of multiple agency activities all impacting on the same audience. This should broaden the agency's restricted view of issues and represents an important transfer of information from the community to agency staff. (Buchy and Hoverman 2000: 22)

Thus, at least in theory, community forestry as policy instrument, as a form of natural resource governance and as a defined management system, should have the capacity to provide a bridge between scientific and non-scientific knowledge and consequently works to diminish cog-nitive conflict. By providing a setting for knowledge exchange, conflict may be acknowledged and eventually addressed.

The community forestry ideal also seeks to promote communi-cation through strong public participation. Communication is the key mechanism for reducing conflicts that arise from misunderstandings causing *false conflicts* (Appelstrand 2002). These are not uncommonly information-based rather than springing from ideological or value-based issues, and can be dissolved through communication, leaving substantive conflict issues (if they exist) to be identified and eventually dealt with (Appelstrand 2002: 287). It may be that after addressing false conflict, there are few if any substantive conflict issues. The basic premise is that mismatched perceptions create misunderstandings that can be resolved through better and ultimately effective communication.

Cognitive conflict can be further reduced by creating a setting capable of incorporating community desires into forest planning and management to find practices that will be better supported by the community. Certainly in several of our cases (British Columbia, the American Southwest and Scandinavia for example) forestry practices have been at the core of conflict – often centered on a negative perception of clear-cuts (clear-felling), range management and grazing practices, or approaches to salvage, and quite irrespective of scientific evidence of positive or negative effects. In contrast community forestry is seen as more environmentally friendly. Community forestry is a *decision-making place* (i.e. a political space as discussed in Chapter 1 of this book) where managers can opt for cut controls very different from the past silvicultural practices, and these controls can better mirror community values than industrial forestry. On the other hand, complexity of community values, and the difficulty of deciding what a community's values are, pose a problem for community forestry. Community forestry may be logging as usual, albeit with a different management structure. As the forest management debate has evolved, chasms have grown within communities where those seeking economic opportunity and stability can find themselves at odds with those who see the community forest as another way of reducing logging, enhancing other opportunities, or manifestly shifting the economic and social foundation of a community away from resource extraction. Whether or not community forestry can address these conflicting expectations is in no small part dependent on context.

Cognitive conflicts arise when decisions are made by distant individuals with perhaps with little sense of place, empathy or understanding of a local area affected by their decisions. Community forestry can enable local decision-making, potentially negating the problems associated with decision-making far removed from the management region. Kimmins (2002: 270) states: "forestry should not be dictated by individuals and groups who are unfamiliar with local ecology, culture, and sociology." It is a perspective that challenges scientific and managerial elitism and remote decision-making, and it is a partial reflection of the long-held view of many communities – that local control will be better because it will be based on local knowledge. But local knowledge may be incomplete, exclusive or selective, or biased. The difficulty with local knowledge is that in some quarters it has taken on a mythical quality – extended as an alternative to science, rather than a form of knowledge that could work with science and other knowledge forms. The *balanced approach* (our term) would seek a better blending of know-ledge-bases and sources (Kimmins 2002). It does not abandon science or professional forestry, but seeks to integrate locally derived knowledge into a more complex process for managing forest resources, focused on local needs and expectations but cognizant of larger environmental and socio-economic contexts. It may be that community forestry provides the location for doing this. No doubt *better* forest management can be achieved by shortening the chain between policy makers and field personnel and by bringing individuals into the management process who are linked to the land through personal history. The effect is to minimize cognitive conflict by reducing "differences between that which is said and that which is done" (Mitchell 1989: 250).

As awareness and knowledge increases, there is a basic human tendency to question what has previously gone unchallenged. There is the potential that community forests could generate cognitive conflict by creating public (cognitive) awareness, and building expectations that cannot be met. The realization that some problems cannot be solved by community forestry because their causes lie elsewhere in the global economy or higher up the administrative ladder can also be agonizing. Community involvement could, therefore, create positive cognitive conflict, challenging the status quo to induce creativity and innovation and to develop new opportunities – some of which may not be based on logging or the forested landscape.

Personal dynamics (values, beliefs and interests)

At the heart of most forest debates lies a conflict over the values that communities hold with respect to basic ideas about forest utilization and the services forests provide, or might provide (Robinson *et al.* 2001: 24). The evolution of forest policy in Canada and the United States has seen the growth of a strong intertwined relationship between govern-ment and industry. At one time this bond, or contract, combined public natural resources with private capital to provide substantial societal benefits. In more recent times, however, government and industry values have come to contrast greatly with new prevalent "public" values that are less tolerant of common industrial practices (Carrow 1994; Robinson *et al.* 2001). Ultimately, such differences lead to questions about the representative nature of government and the accountability of tenure holders. Industry acts in self-interest for corporate shareholder values; however, if the government does not represent public values, then the government cannot rightly serve the public.

In a "perfect world", community forestry would provide the avenue for the incorporation of local values, and the desires of those most immediately affected, into decision-making (Duinker et al. 1991: 134). But misrepresentation leading to conflict can occur if representation on management bodies does not mirror community values and make-up (Appelstrand 2002; Wellstead et al. 2003). From a process perspective, community forests are seen as having great potential to overcome value and belief conflicts, if local representatives are not handpicked solely by industry and government, and if representation is pluralistic and accountable.

Logging and forest industry-based communities across North America, and indeed elsewhere, have experienced serious ecological and social costs, while the majority of financial benefits often leave local supply areas. Moreover, the benefits of forest resource management are not always shared equally within the community. If the conditions of community tenure are that community forest holders *must* manage forest resources in a manner that considers a range of interests in the community, then it is possible to create a setting that can resolve interest conflicts by promoting community-based decision-making, community development, innovation and diversity.

Defining who should be involved, the stakeholders and decision-makers, is a challenge. Conflict can continue and be heightened if the model is too exclusive (Duinker et al. 1994; Clark 2002), or too inclusive. What works best, limited participation or open participation, is context-dependent. Community forestry may not guarantee the equitable distribution of social costs and benefits, neither does community empowerment always lead to democratic resource management; some views and interests can be neglected, while others become dominant (Bradshaw 2003). This also undermines the notion of empowerment in that the distribution of power within the community cannot be equal if some people are not represented. In fact, Appelstrand (2002) suggests that favoritism is less likely to occur when local decision-making processes are free from government intervention and include a wide range and large number of participants.

There is a difference between intervention, which sounds meddling and coercive, and open participation. Community forestry cannot be reasonably implemented in most settings without the cooperation, support and capacities that government brings to the table. Community forestry may not even be possible without changing the institutional structures or legal framework for tenure. Yet a problem to think about is that equal representation might not be realistic owing to the wide variety of local forest interests. For example, this is a concern under cooperative management models where one interest group can physically or psychologically outnumber another in local membership. It cannot be assumed that existing community power relationships will act to support an equal distribution of costs and benefits under a community forest model. Beckley (1998: 742) warns that community forestry may in fact institutionalize conflict "by incorporating sometimes diametrically opposed interests into a single management authority or decision-making body." The result is likely to be a form of social paralysis. Community forests can help to reduce interest conflicts in resource management by better incorporating the concerns of different interest groups in forest management, but their implementation may also create equity and efficiency problems (Beckley 1998).

Furthermore, because the impacts of resource exploitation can extend beyond the spatial and temporal bounds of the community forest, "the interests of people separated from the issue by both space and time" must be taken into consideration (Mitchell 2002: 274). Interest conflicts reach beyond community boundaries and program time frames. Duinker et al. (1994: 717–18) point to a case in the Clayoquot Sound on Vancouver Island, British Columbia, where during the early 1990s efforts to develop a forest management advisory board saw board membership disputed across communities. Clayoquot Sound is legendary in Canada, and indeed abroad, as the poster place for the impacts of logging and the loss of old-growth forests. But such conflicts tend to descend into excessive rhetoric and uncompromising ideologies, and Clayoquot was hardly an exception. Some wanted to log, but do it better, others wanted to preserve trees, and for these interests there was no quarter likely to be given for a timber-based economy. Is a community forest, at least a wholly inclusive one, possible in such contexts? Several communities may "share" a forest region, but they can have very different reasons for supporting a community forest model. Especially at the local level, it is also important to have representative bodies that mirror the community values in order to mitigate conflicts that can challenge implementation efforts. With respect to the design of participation processes, value conflicts can arise at the community level when local actors are selected by senior government and forest industry because the participants do not actually reflect the values, beliefs, behaviors and demographic profile they are supposed to represent (Appelstrand 2002). This can be especially problematic in resource hinterlands where industry and government have a compact and a dominance over activities in a given resource sector. Interest conflicts in resource management may also be linked to temporal considerations and the "intergenerational distribution of costs and benefits" (Dorcey 1986: 39). Achieving representation across generations is certainly a problem that rests on the willingness of participants to be selfless and consider consequences beyond their own lifetime (Mitchell 2002). Communities that manage their own forest resources might be more prepared to make this sacrifice, given their ties to the local area in terms of investment, social commitments and family heritage. Although community forests have mechanisms to address local interest conflicts, external linkages (both spatially and temporally) have also been deemed important enough to influence local decision-making.

This last point has possible implications for community forest tenure holders. Community forests are often sought as a local economic development strategy to empower local people. If interregional and intergenerational conflicts of interest are given further consideration by the courts, then the accountability required to manage a forest may exceed local capacity. In other words, is it reasonable to expect that local community forest managers will be able to manage forest resources for the greatest possible good? The inclusion of these wider conditions also weakens the autonomy of community forest managers and detracts from the notion of independence attached to this form of tenure.

Clearly, the success of community forests to represent their own interests depends on capacity building to form a basis for control. Self-sufficiency is also important to escape the boom and bust economy characteristic of resource towns. Overcoming "shifting forestry" is thought to be achievable under a community forestry model (Duinker *et al.* 1991: 134). But communities do not exist in economic isolation, and in many instances the problems affecting the forest sector are necessarily not supply-based, but have their roots in larger economic trends, lack of product innovation, international competition, and increasing corporate concentration or bad business decisions.

It is important to consider, however, that interest conflicts may surface due to the initial transition from industrial to community tenure. In most cases, decreased timber harvesting will result. For example, in Canada the 2000 British Columbia Forest Policy Review discussed citizen concern regarding the shift to community forest tenure:

there was concern about what [decreased production] might mean for communities and workers. In achieving this strategy there was recognition that some communities might face the loss of high paying jobs as mills reduced activity. This would have significant impacts on the community. There was no agreement on a transition strategy that might be used to mitigate community impacts. (Wouters 2000: 85–6)

Such a transition would inevitably have implications for communities as a whole, though some individuals and groups stand to be more deeply affected than others. There is potential for community forestry to stir interest conflicts regionally, given that some communities will benefit while others are made to feel the costs.

Behavioral conflicts are perhaps the most socially dramatic resource conflicts. They can arise due to any number of reasons, having contemporary and/or historical roots. An example of this might include failed negotiations between a government bureaucracy and discontented Aboriginal groups who refuse to participate in consultation owing to entrenched mistrust from past dealings with governments or others. In North America, and abroad, there have been mass demonstrations against conventional forestry practices. Attempts by industry government and environmental organizations to vilify the opposition can be manifestations of behavioral conflicts, whereby personal feelings of righteous anger color disputes. The intensity of personal emotions and hostilities that can develop makes this an insidious form of conflict, and it may be insurmountable, until the actors are replaced.

It has also been suggested that a "lack of local citizenry involvement in decision-making by a local agency can result in polarized human relationships when things go wrong since 'everybody knows everybody'" (Duinker *et al.* 1994: 718). Such behavioral conflicts are not commonly associated with the dynamics of small-town politics, and may be more typical of rural resource communities. The cultural context of small communities may also seek to enforce a conformity, which makes innovation difficult (Swanson 2001). These perspectives are a tad dire, and ironically, local policy processes that seek to build community-based approaches can do the exact opposite. Alternatively, when things go wrong, a small community may coalesce or have the social capital foundation in place to try "something different" or "move on." In other words, far from having a polarizing effect, the governance setting (based on the qualities of local civil society) is now in place to experiment, respond and implement new ideas or manage change more effectively.

The complex nature of forest management and the interconnectedness of environmental issues make conflict management and planning attractive and necessary. In this vein, community forestry may offer the potential to address what Hanna and Slocombe (2007) call a persistent problem in environmental management – the fragmentation of authority across agencies and jurisdictional levels. But just as fragmentation can be difficult to overcome, even a modest approach to integration can prove challenging to implement.

The characterization of implementation is not conducive to the application of a single template. In community forestry, the implementation process is often hesitant because it is new and begs change to established structures. Sometimes it is ad hoc or adaptive, and it is commonly affected by inconsistencies in budgets, statutory authority, the feral nature of politics, the nuances of public interest, and communication and knowledge. Regular criticisms of environmental agencies are also applicable to forest management agencies. Two familiar refrains center on their role as supporters of industrial forest use and the persistent ineffectiveness of pretty well all bureaucratic structures in addressing pervasive environmental problems (Dryzek 1990; Paehlke 1990; Torgerson 1990). These characteristics are reflected in the fragmented nature of the management processes for land, water, wildlife, and forest resources. Responsibilities for economic, social and environmental management are divided among agencies, or levels of government. Agencies also have established constituencies whose ideologies influence the ability or willingness of administrative structures to implement policy, especially when these may be new or controversial, or counter to the interests of a dominant constituency. Nor are bureaucracies always uniform entities in terms of organization, sense of purpose or internal cohesion. A supportive bureaucracy is essential to implementation, but in some instances bureaucrats will be responsible for putting into effect policies that they have had little influence in formulating or may be viscerally opposed to. So, in the persistent context of fragmentation, who will be responsible for implementing community forestry, or championing it?

There is a growing interest in community forestry, but progress in implementation has been hesitant and unsystematic; even in North America, working examples are few, despite the rich literature and extensive discourse. The community forestry dialogue is perhaps more commonly hopeful rather than reflective of practice reality. In part this hesitancy results from the obstacles outlined here, but it also reflects a reliance on processes where there is no shortage of models, advice and prescriptions but institutional resistance remains. And there is the challenge where community forestry is seen as a problem-solving strategy, injected into already complex situations that are characterized by pervasive conflict (Walther 1987). In this situation, where community forestry is a reactive measure, it may be more likely to succeed as part of a broader proactive approach, where community forestry is one part of a more sophisticated strategy for community sustainability and economic transition and diversification.

Forest management in Canada and the United States can still be characterized as what Skogstad and Kopas (1992: 47) termed a "closed policy network." Bureaucracies can work together and with key non-government interests to develop and implement policy. In many settings, the forest industry has an integral and, perhaps, unduly influential role in policy formulation, operational planning and ongoing decision-making. The relationship between government and the forest industry might be described as client based, where the interests of corporate stakeholders dominate processes (Coleman 1988; Skogstad and Kopas 1992). While resource agencies might include a framework for inter-agency communication and broad public consultation within their mission statement, cooperative multi-party action is rare and can indeed conflict with bureaucratic interests.

Perhaps the greatest challenge in implementing community forestry is not in convincing communities that it is valid, though this can be a challenge too, but rather in achieving a broadly accepted understanding of how to define and implement an approach to forest management that begs all concerned to look at problems and solutions differently and to do things in a new way (Hanna 1999). From a critical perspective, this requires a change in power relationships that may constitute a significant challenge to tractability. Overcoming this challenge requires the construction of settings or places for deliberative practice, without unnecessarily dismantling authority structures, while at the same time making them more attuned to and attentive to community needs and expectations. The cases we provide in this book illustrate the interwoven nature of conflict, communities, their forests, and the implementation of what is a promising but institutionally difficult idea.

REFERENCES

Allan, K. and Frank, D. (1994). Community forests in British Columbia: Models that work. *Forestry Chronicle* **70**(6): 721–4.
Appelstrand, M. (2002). Participation and societal values: The challenge for lawmakers and policy practitioners. *Forest Policy and Economics* **4**(4): 281–90.

Baker, M. and Kusel, J. (2003). *Community Forestry in the United States*, Washington DC: Island Press.

Beckley, T. (1998). Moving toward consensus-based forest management: A comparison of industrial, co-managed, community and small private forests in Canada. *Forestry Chronicle* **74** (5): 736–44.

Bradshaw, B. (2003). Questioning the credibility and capacity of community-based resource management. *Canadian Geographer* **47**(2): 137–50.

Brekke, J.S. (1987). The model-guided method for monitoring program implementation. *Evaluation Review* **11**(3), 281–99.

Briggs, X.S. (1998). Doing democracy up close: Culture, power, and communication in community building. *Journal of Planning Education and Research* **18**: 1–13.

Buchy, M. and Hoverman, S. (2000). Understanding public participation in forest planning: A review. *Forest Policy and Economics* **1**(1): 15–25.

Bullock, R. and Hanna, K. (2008). Community forestry: Mitigating or creating conflict in British Columbia? *Society and Natural Resources* **21**(1): 77–85.

Bullock, R., Hanna, K. and Slocombe, S. (2009). Learning from community forestry experience: Challenges and lessons from British Columbia. *Forestry Chronicle* **85**(2): 293–304.

Carrow, R. (1994). Integrated resource management in Canada – a case study of unrealized potential. *Forestry Chronicle* **70**(1): 19–21.

Clark, T. (2002). *The Policy Process: A Practical Guide for Natural Resource Professionals.* New Haven, CT and London: Yale University Press.

Coleman, W. (1988). *Business and Politics: A Study of Collective Action.* Kingston: McGill-Queen's Press.

Deutsch, M. (1973). *The Resolution of Conflict: Constructive and Destructive Processes.* New Haven, CT: Yale University Press.

Dorcey, A. (1986). *Bargaining in the Governance of Pacific Coastal Resources: Research and Reform.* Vancouver, BC: Westwater Research Centre, University of British Columbia Press.

Dryzek, J.S. (1990). Designs for environmental discourse: The greening of the administrative state. In Paehlke, R. and Torgenson, D. (eds.), *Managing Leviathan*, Peterborough: Broadview.

Duinker, P., Matakala, P., Chege, F. and Bouthillier, L. (1994). Community forestry in Canada: An overview. *Forestry Chronicle* **70**(6): 711–20.

Duinker, P., Matakala, P. and Zhang, D. (1991). Community forestry and its implications for Northern Ontario. *Forestry Chronicle* **67**(2): 131–5.

Easterbrook, S.M., Beck, E.E., Goodlet, J.S. *et al.* (1993). A survey of empirical studies of conflict. In Easterbrook, S. (ed.), *Computer Supported Cooperative Work.* New York: Springer-Verlag, pp. 1–66.

Forester, J. (1999). *The Deliberative Practitioner: Encouraging Participatory Planning Processes.* Cambridge: MIT Press.

Freeman, H. (1980). The present status of evaluation research. In *Evaluating Social Action Projects.* New York: UNESCO, pp. 9–46.

Ham, C. and Hill, M. (1993). *The Policy Process in the Modern Capitalist State.* Toronto: Harvester Wheatsheaf.

Hanna, K. (1999). Integrated resource management in the Fraser River estuary: Stakeholder's perceptions of the state of the river and program influence. *Journal of Soil and Water Conservation* **54**(2): 490–8.

Hanna, K. (2000). The paradox of participation and the hidden role of information. *Journal of the American Planning Association* **66**(4): 398–410.

Hanna, K. and Slocombe, S. (eds.) (2007). *Integrated Resource and Environmental Management: Concepts and Practice.* Toronto: Oxford University Press.

Harvey, S. and Hillier, B. (1994). Community forestry in Ontario. *Forestry Chronicle* **70**(6): 725–30.

Hessing, M. and Howlett, M. (1997). *Canadian Natural Resource and Environmental Policy*. Vancouver, BC: UBC Press.

Hyder, M. (1984). Implementation: The evolutionary model. In Lewis, D. and Wallace, H. (eds.), *Policies into Practice: National and International Case Studies in Implementation*. London: Heinemann Educational Books, pp. 1–18.

Johnson, P. and Duinker, P. (1993). *Beyond Dispute: Collaborative Approaches to Resolving Natural Resources Conflicts*. Thunder Bay, Ontario: Lakehead University, School of Forestry.

Jones, C. (1984). *An Introduction to the Study of Public Policy*. Monterey: Brooks Cole.

Kimmins, J.P. (2002). Future shock in forestry: Where have we come from; where are we going; is there a "right way" to manage forests? Lessons from Thoreau, Leopold, Toffler, Botkin and Nature. *Forestry Chronicle* **78**(2): 263–71.

Kusel, J., Doak, S., Carpenter, S. and Sturtevant, V. (1996). *The Role of the Public in Adaptive Ecosystem Management, Sierra Nevada Ecosystem Project: Final Report to Congress*, Vol II, *Assessment and Scientific Basis for Management Options*. Davis: University of California, Davis, Centres for Water and Wildland Resources.

Linder, S. and Peters, B. (1989). Instruments of government: Perceptions and contexts. *Journal of Public Policy* **9**(1): 35–58.

Margerum, R. and Born, S. (1995). Integrated environmental management: Moving from theory to practice. *Journal of Environmental Planning and Management*. **38**(3): 371–90.

Margerum, R.D. (1999). Getting past yes: From capital creation to action. *Journal of the American Planning Association* **65**(2): 181–92.

Margerum, R.D. and Born, S.M. (2000). A coordination diagnostic for improving integrated environmental management. *Journal of Environmental Planning and Management*. **43**(1), 5–21.

Mazmanian, D. and Sabatier, P. (1981). *Effective Policy Implementation*. Lexington, MA: Lexington Books.

Mitchell, B. (1986). The evolution of integrated resource management. In Lang, R. (ed.), *Integrated Approaches to Resource Management*. Calgary: University of Calgary Press, pp. 13–26.

Mitchell, B. (1989). *Geography and Resource Analysis*, second edition. New York: John Wiley and Sons.

Mitchell, B. (2002). *Resource and Environmental Management*. Harlow, UK and New York: Prentice Hall/Pearson Education.

Paehlke, R. (1990). Democracy and environmentalism: Opening a door to the administrative state. In Paehlke R. and Torgerson, D. (eds.), *Managing Leviathan*. Peterborough: Broadview, pp. 35–58.

Platt, J. (1973). Social traps, *American Psychologist*, August 1973.

Putnam, L. and Poole, M. (1987). Conflict and negotiation. In Jablin, F., Putnam, L., Roberts, K. and Porter, L. (eds.), *Handbook of Organizational Communication*. Newbury Park, CA: Sage, pp. 549–99.

Rayner, S. (1991). A cultural perspective on the structure and implementation of global environmental agreements. *Evaluation Review* **15**(1): 75–102.

Robbins, S. (1989). *Organisational Behaviour: Concepts, Controversies and Applications*. Englewood Cliffs, NJ: Prentice Hall.

Robinson, D., Robson, M. and Rollins, R. (2001). Towards increased influence in Canadian forest management. *Environments* **29**(2): 21–41.

Rossi, P. and Freeman, H. (1985). *Evaluation: A Systemic Approach*. Newbury: Sage.

Skogstad, G. and Kopas, P. (1992). Environmental policy in a federal system: Ottawa and the Provinces. In Boardman, R. (ed.), *Canadian Environmental Policy: Ecosystems, Politics, and Process*. Toronto: Oxford, pp. 43–59.

Swanson, L. (2001). Rural policy and direct local participation: Democracy, inclusiveness, collective agency and locality-based policy. *Rural Sociology* **66**(1): 1–21.

Teitelbaum, S., Beckley, T. and Nadeau, S. (2006). A national portrait of community forestry on public land in Canada. *Forestry Chronicle* **82**(3): 416–28.

Torgerson, D. (1990). Obsolescent Leviathan: Problems of order in administrative thought. In Paehlke, R. and Torgerson, D. (eds.), *Managing Leviathan*. Peterborough: Broadview, pp. 17–34.

Van Meter, D. and Van Horn, C. (1975). The policy implementation process: A conceptual framework. *Administration and Society* **6**(4): 445–88.

Walther, P. (1987). Against idealistic beliefs in the problem solving capacities of integrated resource management. *Environmental Management* **11**(4): 439–46.

Weale, A. (1992). Implementation failure: A suitable case for review? In Lykke, E. (ed.), *Achieving Environmental Goals: The Concept and Practice of Environmental Performance Review*. London: Belhaven Press, pp. 43–66.

Wellstead, A., Richard, S. and John, P. (2003). Understanding the concept of representation within the context of local forest management decision making. *Forest Policy and Economics* **5**(1): 1–11.

Wouters, G. (2000). *Shaping our Future: BC Forest Policy Review*. Victoria, BC: British Columbia Ministry of Forests.

3

Keeping New England's forests common

In this chapter we elaborate how some communities have become part of the fabric of forest management in the northeastern United States. The New England region contains the oldest community forests from the European tradition in North America.[1] There is a strong tradition of community forests in New England with roots dating back to the forest commons imported by English colonial settlers during the mid 1600s (see McCullough 1995; Donahue 1999). The region also has a longstanding history of municipally owned local private land holdings, which have been assembled since about the mid 1800s as lands were gradually gifted, purchased or annexed with changing land ownership and conservation priorities. For its efforts, New England is recognized for its role "in both historic maintenance as well as recent establishment of town or municipal community forests" (Belsky 2008: 223).

The heritage of common and town forests has fostered a shared mindset founded on shared access to forests and forest benefits, as well as a habitual familiarity with the notion of having community forests on the landscape. Some suggest there is a tradition of community forest stewardship that transcends the spirit of "individuality and self-sufficiency" for which New Englanders are known (Northern Community Forestry Center 2003: 4). The recent proliferation of community-based conservation groups continues the quest to preserve open spaces by conserving both recreational and working landscapes. It might be argued that such a basic appreciation for and commitment to local stewardship, and keeping New England's forests common, provides an important base that in part supports the individual freedoms of community members.

McCullough (1995) provides the seminal work on the history and nature of communal forests in New England. He notes that early European settlers imported the vision of having a village commons:

43

"Excluding native American settlements, New England's first villages were a blend of economic enterprise and utopian idealism, in which extensive forest and open lands became communal resources, shared in both ownership and use" (McCullough 1995: 14–15). McCullough questions whether a "communal spirit" led to the persistence of forest commons across New England towns or whether this collective mindset is due to some other interplay of shifting societal values and land-use pressures. He does highlight, for example, that towns founded by early survey for the quick division and sale of land are not characterized by tracts of commonly held lands. Indeed, the creation of communal forests may have contributed to and reinforced a shared identity and common sense of place where appreciation for collective access to and returns from forest lands were engrained in local culture.

Drawing from communal, town forest, and community-based conservation examples in the northeastern United States, we describe here the roles of town and state governments, non-government organizations and local landowners, and link them to broader concepts of community control and land ownership.

COMMUNAL FORESTS

New England's communal forests were created when the early colonial government granted lands through town charters to groups of people for the establishment of towns to promote settlement. At the time responsibility for town planning was essentially placed on town proprietors – individuals who organized surveying and construction boundaries, house lots, roads and community buildings. Surrounding residual lands remained commonly owned where individual rights to use were subject to collective rules for use and abuse (McCullough 1995: 14–15). Common lands were collectively designated by the townspeople for grazing, cultivation and woodlots based on site characteristics (e.g. location, drainage, forest cover, slope, nearness to water).

As populations were small, the pressure on resources was quite low and so common resources were not in much jeopardy of widespread overexploitation or capture by private individuals or groups (Belsky 2008). Citizens agreed to certain conditions on timber use, namely there would be free access to timber for use in town by local residents, and local wood was not to benefit those beyond town boundaries (i.e. not to be "exported"). These common institutions were infused by a spirit of collective ownership and stewardship as well as protectionist values to ensure maximum local benefit – the latter of which emanated from emerging communities of citizens focused inward on their shared "spiritual confrontation" of the New England wilderness (McCullough 1995: 14–15).

The early period of colonial settlement focused on meeting basic lifestyle needs and wants of town constituents and developing a meaningful economy based on common land and timber resources remained a secondary priority. However, as towns and their administrative systems evolved common resources were used to create public benefits. Sale or taxation of wood products taken from common land helped to meet common expenses (McCullough 1995: 29). For example, taxes were levied against trees harvested for specific uses, ranging from masts to barrels, floor boards, shingles and fencing material. And as the timber industry expanded, professional loggers, surveyors and people to monitor harvesting were soon hired for common woodlot operations.

A combination of driving factors eventually provided the impetus for the "subtle but relentless transformation of common land from a communal resource to a commodity belonging to a select group of town members" (McCullough 1995: 30). Population growth and industry expansion threatened to deplete common forest resources, and the high value of cleared land (for agriculture) put pressure on town proprietors to sell off to private holdings. Town proprietors and their individual wealth (themselves antecedents of a privileged "landed class") were increasingly resented by incoming inhabitants seeking to benefit from undivided forest lands. After all, proprietors were solely responsible for conditions until towns became incorporated. The demands of squatters, limited control of some absentee proprietors and the increasing political organization at the town level further challenged the proprietary system of government.

Increasingly, towns came to represent broader interests, and united citizens soon supplanted former individual proprietary interests. Consequently, forest commons were designated as public lands severed from proprietary control (McCullough 1995: 34). This included lands obtained for the church and minister, schools and the general public which became central to town planning and institutions. For example, town poor farms provided a source of community welfare for aged, poor and sick people, although the stigma of residing there was less positive. Such lands were used for livestock, lumber and crops. The social role and productivity of town farms declined by the end of the nineteenth century as senior governments assumed increased responsibility for public welfare. While some town farms were sold off to private interests, many towns actively maintained woodlot management and later converted

these woodlots and pastures into town forests during the town forest
movement in the early twentieth century (McCullough 1995).

Vestiges of some original forest commons do remain on New
England's forest landscape. One such example is the town of Conway,
New Hampshire which owns and manages about 1840 acres (or 750
hectares) of town forest lands, about half of which originates from
the *Conway Common Lands* (Community Forest Collaborative 2007).
Much of the remaining Common Lands is located high above the town
site on Hurricane Mountain, and many residents today enjoy the familiar aesthetics and recreational opportunities provided by the town-
owned Whitaker Woods in the valley below, unaware of this common
forest legacy.

THE "TOWN FOREST" MOVEMENT

New England's Town Forest movement, and the expansion of municipal
ownership and management of forests, were driven by growing public
awareness of natural resource depletion and degradation caused by
land clearing for agriculture and development. The first town forest
was formally established in 1710 by the town selectmen of Newington,
New Hampshire to protect natural resources from overuse and development (McBane and Barrett 1986). However, the main thrust of the town
forest movement began during the mid 1880s as municipal representatives were increasingly concerned for the loss of taxes and non-
productivity of abandoned farms and cutovers. Such degraded and
"idle" lands represented a burden for local decision-makers (McCullough 1995). By 1880, land clearing for agriculture and pasture had
reached its height and New England's stony, infertile lands were quickly
becoming economically and ecologically inoperable (Irland 1999). In
many ways the town forest movement can be seen as coupled with
the emergence of the North American conservation movement. Credit
for the development of policies and programs to enable the creation of
town forests, and the associated professional and technical competencies to help administer and manage such forests, is owed to the work of
local leaders, service groups, forestry professionals and associations,
non-government organizations and policy makers.

Realizing the need to understand the scale of the deforestation
problem, each New England state formed commissions to compile
forest data as a first step towards assessing the overall state of forest
lands (McCullough 1995: 116–28). Despite the fact that New England
towns had long owned woodlots, there was no supporting policy or law

at the state level that allowed local authorities to purchase – and profit from – private lands. In 1882, Massachusetts was the first state to create legislation that recognized a role for towns in forest management and timber production and, importantly, the link between forest land management and protecting water resources. Maine and New Hampshire soon followed, so that by 1915 enabling legislation was in place to help towns to acquire and manage woodlands. As McCullough (1995: 128) points out, the enactment of this legislation marks the formal beginning of the town forest movement. Responding to rising public concerns for resource conservation, New England towns sought to acquire lands to secure reservoirs, headwaters and adjacent lands for management and remediation. It was during this period that the New England states established a system of nurseries and fire suppression, and each appointed a state forester and pursued policies supporting government purchase of forested lands for public reserves and parks.

Associations and forestry professionals also played key roles (McCullough 1995). The newly formed Massachusetts Forestry Association (MFA) and Society for the Protection of New Hampshire Forests (SPNHF) together promoted the establishment of local forestry organizations, local forest staff and public forestry awareness to push for new forestry legislation. Concerned with unrestricted logging on private land, maintaining public access and conservation in general, the SPNHF specifically was created by political figures to pursue the public takeover of "forests and important scenic areas" (McCullough 1995: 118–19). Their actions contributed to the formation of the 1911 *Weeks Act* which created the White Mountain Forest Reserve. Importantly, the legislation enabled the federal government to purchase privately owned land to protect the headwaters of navigable streams and in doing so, set aside lands with multiple use values for nearby towns (Lavigne 2003). Bernard Fernow, founder and director of University of Toronto's forestry school and himself a prominent figure of the conservation movement, addressed the SPNHF in 1913 to advocate the need for state-led programs to provide funding and expertise for the creation of town forests (McCullough 1995).

Curiously, the same debates surrounding the viability and benefits of community forests today were simmering among advocates and opponents of the town forest movement a century ago. For example, there were concerns about the implications of converting private taxable lands to public town forests, which persist today in New Hampshire and Maine (personal communication, W. Scribner, June 2009). Eligible town forest lands were often marginal lands to begin with (i.e. often

Table 3.1 *Distribution and growth of town forests during the mid-1920s**

State	Period	Number/increase	Acreage
Massachusetts	1924–1930	28–90	25,500
New Hampshire	1925–1930	61–79	16,000
Vermont	1926–1930	33–42	9,000
Maine	1930	30	–

*Based on data from McCullough (1995: 154)

remote, socially contentious, formerly logged, and not suitable for agriculture owing to steep terrain, poor soils and drainage), which brought profitability into question and made these lands difficult to manage. The long delay between the costs of regeneration and future revenues also challenged support for town forests (McCullough 1995). Local concerns for the significance and timing of financial return on investment from community forests persist today (see Bullock 2006, 2007).

However, proponents emphasized a number of benefits such as public education and opportunities for public service. A number of demonstration farms were providing farmers and other land owners with technical examples on how to grow the best timber according to local site conditions, which promoted forest stewardship; under the general label of employment it was suggested that town forests served as training grounds for young foresters, and a source of work for unskilled laborers as well as employment for bush laborers during the doldrums of the employment off-season (McCullough 1995). Town forests also provided relief and fuel wood for the poor as well as commercial timber revenues for the town. "Municipal forestry thus became part of a broad plan to stabilize local economies through forestry education and example" (McCullough 1995: 144–8). According to McCullough's estimates, numerous town forests were established in the early to mid 1920s (Table 3.1), encouraged by a steady wave of promotional literature and support in the form of donated trees, planting labor and technical expertise from various state departments, associations, service clubs and industry.

The town forest movement established a pattern of acquisition and planting concentrated on Massachusetts, New Hampshire and Vermont to a lesser extent until about 1930 (McCullough 1995). Support for town forests swelled once again when the US Forest Service introduced a community forest program in 1938. The number of town forests in Vermont, Maine and Connecticut increased for a brief period during this time. However, the federal government played only a passive role in supporting town forests and local control, characterized by a reluctance to interfere with local interests and "vague skepticism about the ability of towns and charitable organizations to manage profitable forests" (McCullough 1995: 186).

The town forest movement wound down through the 1940s and 1950s. The hardships of the depression and World War II shifted emphasis from acquisition and planting to maintaining existing forest holdings. At the same time the Massachusetts Forestry Association and other champion organizations shifted their promotional efforts from town forest creation to broader conservation initiatives. The termination of federal community forestry programs and community forest committees by national forestry associations during the early 1950s marked the close of the town forest movement (McCullough 1995).

CONSERVING OPEN SPACE THROUGH PUBLIC–PRIVATE–CIVIC COLLABORATION

McCullough's (1995) historical analysis of the early town forest movement highlights the different combinations of values and actors that contributed to the formation of town forests:

> As a movement, town forests grew from escalating interests in forest conservation and pursued the goal of timber cultivation through sustained yield management. Yet motives for establishing forests varied from town to town and often evinced a collaborative effort between town committees and forestry associations or state foresters. (McCullough 1995: 132)

The town forest movement gave way to – or set the stage for – an increasingly complex array of multi-party arrangements and values seeking to conserve open space that can be seen to represent quasi-public community forests in New England. The increasingly high percentage of privatization and amenity values sought by a growing population of suburban residents throughout New England has raised concerns for ongoing public access to rural and recreational forests. Increasing pressure on land use, and shifting societal values and attitudes, have created social conflict between local rural residents and suburban amenity migrants and seasonal visitors holding what Irland (1982: 11) called a "suburban attitude toward land – as a commodity for private use and not as a community asset." A new range of players and tactics has emerged through civil, private and public cooperation to combat the privatization and fragmentation of locally significant open lands by "outside" development interests.

Community-based conservation organization forests (Belsky 2008) represent one approach used to secure and conserve open lands that hold significant aesthetic, cultural, ecological and/or economic values for nearby communities. Community forests established under this model are "owned or managed by community-based or affiliated non-profit conservation organizations frequently collaborating or partnering with other non-profit groups, landowners, local or regional land trusts and state or federal resource-management agencies" (Belsky 2008: 224). In particular, land trusts and foundations have become key players in maintaining local control and management of forest lands by facilitating the strategic purchase and donation of lands or easements for community and family forests that would otherwise be developed for private use. The stories of two initiatives are briefly described below to illustrate the role of land trusts and different combinations of actors involved in conserving open spaces.

The Freedom Town Forest, New Hampshire

The Freedom Town Forest was created in June 2005 after 4 years of work by local residents to protect a 2,661-acre (or about 1,075-hectare) private forest property, treasured for its recreational and unique ecological values (Freedom Town Forest 2008). Unassumingly known as "Trout Pond," the property was at the center of an ongoing controversy involving the landowner, who planned to develop the property, and local officials and residents who wanted to conserve it for open space and to maintain "public" access (personal communication, R. Gerard, June 2009) (Figure 3.1). While this was not a formal public green space, locals from the towns of Freedom and Madison had long treated it as such, enjoying open access to the woods (a local practice common to both Denman and Cortes Islands in British Columbia, as discussed in Chapter 6 of this book).

From an ecological point of view, Trout Pond's location in the Ossipee Watershed and position over New Hampshire's largest stratified drift aquifer made it important for town drinking-water supplies. The property also contained a rare and threatened Pine Barren ecosystem. Together with adjacent conservation lands (i.e. Madison Town Forest and Nature Conservancy's West Branch Pine Barrens Preserve), Trout Pond helped to form a 5,800-acre (or about 2,350-hectare) open space and wildlife corridor (Freedom Town Forest 2008).

Figure 3.1 The 21-acre Trout Pond, Freedom Town Forest, New Hampshire (photo: R. Bullock).

When the land owner encountered financial difficulty, and plans for luxury development failed, local conservation group the Friends of Trout Pond joined forces with Green Mountain Conservation Group, the Town of Freedom, the State of New Hampshire and The Trust for Public Land to pursue the opportunity to purchase Trout Pond using both public and private funds. Town and local fundraising monies were combined with grants from New Hampshire's Land and Community Heritage Investment Program (LCHIP) as well as the USDA Forest Legacy Program, which supports state efforts for the protection of private and environmentally sensitive forest lands from non-forest use and development (USDA 2011). Owned by the Town of Freedom, the property was conserved through an easement owned by the State of New Hampshire (Freedom Town Forest 2008).

The stated mission of the Freedom Town Forest is to "maintain the forest, in perpetuity, as open space for the enjoyment and education of the public" (Freedom Conservation Commission 2007). The Freedom Town Forest is managed under a plan prepared by the consulting forester. Use regulations are visibly posted to advise community members on accepted uses. The tradition of multiple use continues through forest and wildlife management, and recreation activities such as hunting, fishing and hiking; however, overnight camping, fires, target shooting and removal of forest materials are

Figure 3.2 Lacroix Farm and Family Forest on the Mad River and Route 100B near Moretown, Vermont (photo: R. Bullock).

restricted. Timber harvesting does occur on a sustainable basis, mainly for site and habitat improvement, with timber revenues flowing to the town.

(Bruce) Lacroix Farm and Family Forest, Moretown, Vermont

The public benefits derived from private property are not always obvious. However, the story of how the Lacroix Farm and Family Forest was established illustrates how a private land transaction can be purposefully designed to pursue personal interests, while ensuring that wider community values are upheld.

In 2007, the Bruce family decided that it might be time to sell their intergenerational dairy farm in the Mad River Valley near Moretown, Vermont. Neither the owners nor local residents took the decision lightly. The 102-acre farm (about 41 hectares) had been in the valley, and in the Bruce family, for a century. The large pasture and wooded mountainsides were prominent features of the scenic landscape along Route 100B (Figure 3.2). Given its scenic location and proximity to nearby ski resorts, the Bruce family feared the agricultural lands and woods would be lost to development if they could not find the "right" buyer. They approached the Vermont Land Trust (VLT) to explore options for conserving the farm.

Around the same time, fellow Vermonters and organic farmers Keith and Rae-anne Lacroix had been searching for a working property to scale up from their existing operation. The Lacroixes themselves had previously applied to VLT competitions for other farms, but had been unsuccessful given the steep competition among the farming community (personal communication, K. Lacroix, June 2009). The Lacroixes received a major break when they learned through word of mouth that the Bruce family had approached VLT. The Lacroixes decided to contact the Bruce family directly about the unlisted property. After touring the property together for an hour, the Bruce family signaled their approval of the Lacroixes' vision by offering to sell them the farm.

As young farmers the Lacroixes told the Bruce family outright: "We can't afford this place unless it goes to be conserved" (personal communication, K. Lacroix, June 2009). The Bruce family liked the Lacroixes' plan to produce organic vegetables, eggs and grass-fed beef and to open a cooperative farm stand in one of the historic farm buildings. However, the Bruce brothers also knew that their deceased father would not have liked the idea of selling the development rights (W. Bruce, personal communication, June 2009). Yet there was alignment between the interests and values held by both families. Neither family wanted to see another "Mc-mansion" on the landscape, or the possible subdivision of productive agricultural land. "You want a white farm house and a red barn. That's what everyone thinks when you say 'Vermont'" (personal communication, K. Lacroix, June 2009). A farmer-to-farmer agreement was struck that started a 2-year land transaction involving both families, and eventually the VLT and Vermont Housing and Conservation Board (VHCB). When community members heard that a deal was in progress to conserve the Bruce property, local businesses, churches and private citizens among others contributed to VLT fundraising efforts to show community support for the small farm and the Lacroixes' plan to start a community market.

The purchase of the farm was made possible by the simultaneous sale of the development rights. The property was essentially divided into two plots: the open farmland and adjacent woods. VHCB conserved the development rights and placed an agricultural easement on the 37-acre (15-hectare) working farmland, while the 65-acre (26-hectare) wood-lot was placed in the VLT under a conservation easement. The Lacroixes hired a consulting forester to prepare a management plan for the woods as a condition of conservation easement. The land transfer was completed in spring 2009.

The deal worked on many levels. It contributed to maintaining farming viewscapes important not only to locals but to Vermont's tourism economy in general. It conserved significant frontage on the Mad River, riparian habitat and adjacent hill slope forest. It conserved an agricultural property that would contribute directly to local food production and create opportunity for emerging organic farmers. Overall, conserving this iconic private property helped to maintain a common way of life and a community culture that typifies Vermont life and economy.

SUMMARY

New England's early settlement history, town conservation and planning efforts, and non-government organizations created a legacy of town-owned land. The early abandonment of farmland contributed to efforts to restore forest cover before the rest of the country had reached a similar stage of forestry issues (Irland 1999). For better or worse, the town forest movement was well under way by the time the North American conservation movement took hold.

As seen above, community forests in New England are not black and white cases of publicly owned forests used for multiple values and benefits. Private ownership by towns, resident families and individuals; land trusts and easements; government programs and state departments all played (and play) a role in keeping New England's forests common. The outcome is a mosaic of working and recreation-based forests; all the values associated with community forests are present but they are emphasized more or less in one situation than another. Evolving combinations of ideas and actions by private–civic–public actors have created several variations of what can be seen as community forests – town-owned conservation lands, multi-stakeholder stewardship partnerships, state-held easements on private working and amenity landscapes, and publicly owned forest reserves and protected areas. In each case the ecosystems services provided cannot be bound to a single property. All are part of efforts to conserve the common forests and open spaces of New England.

NOTE

1 We acknowledge that the indigenous peoples of North America practice various forms of community forestry that have evolved since time immemorial.

REFERENCES

Belsky, J. (2008). Creating community forests. In Donoghue, E. and Sturtevant, V. (eds.). *Forest Community Connections: Implications for Research, Management, and Governance.* Washington: Resources for the Future Press, pp 219–42.

Bullock, R. (2006). An analysis of community forest implementation in British Columbia Canada. Unpublished MES thesis. Wilfrid Laurier University, Waterloo, Ontario.

Bullock, R. (2007). Two sides of the forest. *Journal of Soil and Water Conservation* **62**(1): 12A–15A.

Community Forest Collaborative (2007). *Community Forests: A Community Investment Strategy.* A report by the Community Forest Collaborative.

Donahue, B. (1999). *Reclaiming the Commons.* New Haven, CT: Yale University Press.

Freedom Conservation Commission (2007). *Freedom Town Forest Regulations. RSA 31:112, RSA 41:11.* New Hampshire: Freedom Conservation Commission.

Freedom Town Forest (2008). *Freedom Town Forest Backgrounder.* Freedom Town Forest, NH.

Irland, L. (1982). *Wildlands and Woodlots: The Story of New England's Forests.* Hanover, NH: University Press of New England.

Irland, L. (1999). *The Northeast's Changing Forest.* Petersham, MA: Harvard University Press.

Lavigne, P. (2003). Community forestry at the urban–rural interface: The Beaver Brook Association and the Merrimack River Watershed. In Kusel, J. and Adler, E. (eds.) *Forest Communities, Community Forests.* Oxford, UK: Rowman and Littlefield, pp. 257–80.

McBane, C. and Barrett, J. (1986). *Town forest and community life: A management guide. Research Report Number 109.* Durham, New England: New Hampshire Agricultural Experiment Station, University of New Hampshire.

McCullough, R. (1995). *Landscape of Community: A history of Communal Forests in New England.* Hanover, NH: University of New England Press.

Northern Community Forestry Center (2003). *Engaging Residents in Planning for Municipal Forests: A Case Study of Lincoln, Vermont.* Northern Community Forestry Center, Northern Forest Region.

USDA (2011). Forest Legacy Program. Available at http://www.fs.fed.us/spf/coop/programs/loa/flp.shtml. Accessed June 1, 2011.

4

Experiments and false starts: Ontario's community forestry experience

Relative to other Canadian regions, the province of Ontario has a long experience with community forests. Since the early 1900s, policies and programs enabling local control of forests have been pursued across levels of government, yet oftentimes with hesitance, despite a relatively long and successful experience with models of local control. The concept has been frequently revisited during times of heightened public concern for ecological degradation, social conflict and economic disaster when it seemed a unique or experimental institutional response was needed.

Proliferation of community forests in southern Ontario had much to do with historic patterns of settlement and land use, and core–periphery dynamics between the provincial south and north respectively. Over time a conventional company town culture has evolved based on industrial use and control of forest resources concentrated in the provincial north. Conversely, the southern portion of the province is both more urban and agricultural, and conservation-oriented.

This chapter examines prominent local control models developed in Ontario. We present the ecological and socio-political contexts from which different forms of community forests emerged and discuss experiences across programmatic, geographical and cultural settings. Various factors, namely reforestation, community and regional development, and First Nations and public involvement have elevated government and social group interest in community forests periodically. Below we provide a brief historical sketch and overview of prominent models of community forests in Ontario (Table 4.1), namely the:

- Agreement Forest Program;
- Algonquin Forest Authority;
- Wendaban Stewardship Authority;

Table 4.1 *Basic characteristics of different community forest models in Ontario*

Name and origin	Mean* or total+ land holdings (ha)	Land ownership	Enabling legislation or agreement	Organizational model	Primary funding sources
Agreement Forests (1922)	2,000*	Private land owned by county, township or municipality	Agreement Forest Act; Crown Forest Sustainability Act	Partnership of landowner and manager; local board	Provincial
Conservation Authorities (1946)	143,000+	Private land owned by municipal body	Conservation Authorities Act	Municipal–provincial funding and technical partnership, corporation of watershed municipalities with appointed board	Provincial and federal transfers; municipal levy, other sources (charity)
Algonquin Forest Authority (1974)	288,886+	Crown land (provincial park)	Algonquin Forest Authority Act; Crown Forest Sustainability Act	Crown corporation with appointed board	Logging revenues
Wendaban Stewardship Authority (1990)	130,000+	Crown land (& provincial park)	Memorandum of Understanding between First Nation and Province	Shared stewardship board including provincial (2/3) and First Nation (1/3) appointees	Various licenses, permits, fees from land/resource use

Table 4.1 (cont.)

Name and origin	Mean* or total+ land holdings (ha)	Land ownership	Enabling legislation or agreement	Organizational model	Primary funding sources
Ontario Community Forest Pilot Program (1991)	323,500*	Crown land and unceded Indian Reserve land	Crown Forest Sustainability Act	Mixed: partnerships and non-profit corporations with appointed and elected interest group representation, ranging from one to six communities; land and resource committee accountable to Chief and Council	Provincial, logging, organizational programs/services
Westwind Stewardship Incorporated (1996)	360,000+	Crown land	Crown Forest Sustainability Act	Non-profit corporation with board of elected at-large community and interest group members	Charity, forest industry, logging and services

- Ontario Community Forest Pilot Program; and
- Westwind Stewardship Incorporated.

Attention is given to the main characteristics such as mandated object-ives, organizational structure and funding arrangements, as well as their documented successes, challenges and opportunities going for-ward. What emerges is a record of relative success, yet ongoing provin-cial resistance to the concept of local control over resources. This has had much to do with the power relations and competing visions, as well as unforeseeable events shaping how Ontario forest policies, economies and communities have developed.

APPROACHES TO COMMUNITY FORESTRY IN ONTARIO

The Agreement Forest Program, 1922–2001

Ontario's Agreement Forest Program began in 1922 and represents the longest experience (80 years) with local government involvement in public land management following European settlement in Canada. Much of the early policy momentum for creating Agreement Forests is owed to the collective concern of farmers, foresters, rural politicians and civil society (including such organizations as the Ontario Fruit Growers Association) who together observed first hand and reported on the effects of extensive deforestation on soil and water resources (Ontario Ministry of Natural Resources, OMNR 1986). Origins of the program date back as early as 1871, when Ontario introduced legisla-tion authorizing municipalities to partially fund landowners for tree planting, with up to 50% reimbursement from the province. Of primary motivation was the need to rehabilitate degraded and abandoned farm-lands and cutover forest lands – the "waste barrens" of southern Ontario, resulting from "misguided settlement" and poor land-use management practices (e.g. logging, tilling, burning). Topsoils were being washed away by rain and blowsands in some instances came to cover areas greater than 30 hectares (75 acres). The removal of vegeta-tion exacerbated drought conditions in farmlands and spring flooding downstream in urban areas (OMNR 1986).

Just as in the eastern United States at the time (Chapter 3 in this book), idle and abandoned lands were greatly devalued and often became the burden of municipal governments. Ongoing forest clear-ance for agriculture contributed to erosion to the point where farming and logging no longer provided a sustainable way to generate liveli-hoods (Richardson 1974). In 1896, a tax assessment-based survey of forest area in 35 counties in southern Ontario indicated that there was a vast area of non-productive wastes, some 949,000 hectares (nearly 2,350,000 acres) or almost 16% of the region (Armson 2001). Noteworthy is that this early survey underestimated land clearance for southern Ontario, given that it did not cover several key agricultural counties (e.g. Essex, Norfolk, Haldimand). There was also the issue of data accuracy, considering that some cost-conscious farmers tended to underestimate their amounts of taxable land.

By 1908 there was an estimated 65,000 hectares (160,000 acres) of public land being reforested thanks to earlier provincial reforestation legislation (Zavitz 1909). Nonetheless, ongoing concern for the growing economic burden associated with idle and acquired abandoned farmlands led the Ontario legislature to pass the *Counties Reforestation Act* in 1911, which enabled counties to buy land for development, management and planting (Zavitz 1909). To provide additional incentive for reforestation, the province passed the 1922 *Reforestation Act*. In addition to purchasing land, the Reforestation Act further enabled counties to enter into agreements with the provincial Ministry of Lands and Forests, which would in turn carry out the planting and management of the forest at its own expense (OMNR 1986). Agreements were typically for 20 to 50 years, and could be renewed or responsibility would revert to the counties for the cost of development, less Crown revenues generated from the land base during the agreement period. Four years after the Agreement Forest Program was introduced, 1,600 hectares across four counties were under agreement (OMNR 1986).

The *Forestry Act* of 1927 replaced the Reforestation Act and expanded the Agreement Forest Program to include "firms, corporations or municipal corporations, as well as persons." The expansion later brought Conservation Authorities, the federal government National Capital Commission and one forest company (Domtar) into agreements. Additional legislative changes in the mid 1940s and later 1960s made it possible for townships and municipalities, respectively, to enter agreements (OMNR 1986), and also larger population centers such as cities with over 10,000 people. By 1960, over 75,000 hectares (185,000 acres) of county and township forest areas and another 19,000 hectares (47,000 acres) of Conservation Authority forest areas were under agreement (Zavitz 1909). The Agreement Forest Program eventually grew to include 111,000 hectares (274,000 acres) and 54 owners by the mid 1980s (OMNR 1986). Only two of these forests were located in northern Ontario (i.e. Bonfield Township and Lakehead Region

Conservation Authority), the rest being concentrated in the southern urban–agricultural region of Ontario.

Agreement Forests evolved from plantations intended for soil rehabilitation (Zavitz 1909). However, embrace of the multiple use paradigm, shifting societal values and ongoing redefinition of terminology in the Forestry Act (specifically the term "forestry purposes") caused a broadening of their mandate to include wood and wood-product production, wildlife habitat, flood and erosion control, recreation and water supply. Following preparation of a management plan approved by the landowner, the province undertook a variety of activities in keeping with a multiple use approach including tree planting, forest stand improvement, and the construction of roads, trails, fencing, recreation areas and ponds, as well as erosion control and habitat work (OMNR 1986). Evolving from the early focus on reforestation, Agreement Forests also became important sites for outdoor education and forest research.

Agreement Forests were based on a partnership model consisting of a landowner (primarily local government) and a forest manager (i.e. OMNR). While the province was responsible for management and funding, lands were owned fee simple by a local government organization. To assist counties, regional municipalities, townships and Conservation Authorities to acquire lands, OMNR could grant up to 75% of the land value and legal fees. In such cases land could not be sold without Ministry approval and/or sharing of land sales revenues (OMNR 1986). The area under agreement could also change over time and when managed for recreation primarily, revenues and expenses were not charged against the forest but covered by the Ministry and agreement holder as current expenditures. There was also no charge to the land owner for planted trees. OMNR paid expenses and was authorized to generate and collect revenues from agreement lands, and fiscal accountability was maintained through annual financial records and reporting (OMNR 1986). As community forests, Agreement Forest decision-making was (and is) directed by a local government body consisting of elected representatives that typically contains individuals with little to no forestry expertise. Decision-makers tend to focus on finances, administration and policy, leaving daily operational decisions to hired forestry staff (Teitelbaum *et al.* 2006).

The Agreement Forest model has evolved differently according to local ecological, economic and administrative contexts. This is perhaps best demonstrated by the observed variability in management efforts across Agreement Forests (Teitelbaum *et al.* 2006). A main strength of the model is that forest land is owned outright, providing, in theory, maximum flexibility for management, use and local input. Yet Teitelbaum *et al.* (2006) observe that in some cases where management responsibility lies with local government representatives, Agreement Forest councils and residents can be unaware of or even indifferent to management decisions, and very little happens in these forests in terms of active management and even recreation. Conversely, some Agreement Forests have a strong record of recreation, education, wetland and wildlife protection, and harvesting complete with advisory and consultation processes to solicit public input.

One drawback is that Agreement Forest owners and managers must deal with a fragmented forest land base that tends to be smaller and less profitable than community forests found in other provinces. According to a survey of community forests across Canada (Teitelbaum *et al.* 2006), 40% of Ontario Agreement Forests claimed to be self-sufficient, though much of this success was admittedly achieved through limiting the resources earmarked for management in the first place. Teitelbaum *et al.* (2006) also found that there was limited success with engaging First Nations in operational and management planning decisions. In part, this may be due to the concentration of Agreement Forests in southern Ontario where there are fewer Aboriginal communities than in the provincial north. However, 2006 census-based estimates report that many Aboriginal people do live in southern Ontario – almost 49% (or 143,150 people) – although, evidently, not in Aboriginal communities (Ontario Ministry of Community and Social Services, OMCSS 2008).

A period of neo-conservative politics during the mid 1990s led to significant downsizing and cuts in the budgets of provincial resource and environmental management agencies. This led the OMNR to download management and administrative responsibility for Agreement Forests to municipal and regional government organizations once again (Teitelbaum *et al.* 2006). Fifteen years after the Agreement Forest program, 50 Agreement Forests remain, 24 of which are managed by counties, regional municipalities and lone municipalities, and the other 26 by Conservation Authorities.

The Algonquin Forest Authority/Agence de foresterie du parc Algonquin, 1974 to present

The Algonquin Forest Authority/Agence de foresterie du parc Algonquin was created to reduce conflict in Canada's oldest provincial park.

Algonquin Park was created in 1893 upon recommendation from the Royal Commission on Forest Reservation and National Park to protect it from settlement and unrestricted logging. However, logging continued in the park so that by 1960 there were 20 logging licenses feeding forest-product industries in several towns surrounding the park. These competing land uses contributed to a public controversy surrounding the future of the park and local economy. This led to the development of a provisional master plan for the park in 1968, which attempted to segregate uses (zoning approach). This planning process would turn out to be instrumental because it provided a forum for debate and resulted in a revised master plan in 1974, which established the Algonquin Forest Authority (AFA) in 1974 under special circumstance and legislation (AFA 2010; P.J. Usher Consulting Services, PJUCS 1994).

The Algonquin Forest Authority's objectives are:

(a) to harvest Crown timber and produce logs therefrom and to sort, sell, supply and deliver the logs;

(b) to perform, undertake and carry out such forestry, land management and other programs and projects as the Minister may authorize and to advise the Minister on forestry and land management programs and projects of general advantage to Ontario. Revised Statutes of Ontario 1990, c.A.17, s.9(1)

The AFA became the sole license, replacing numerous previous private licenses that benefited populations in several towns on the park perimeter. Existing forest companies retained their ministerial fiber commitments, which are specified in the Algonquin Park Forestry Agreement with the responsible Ministry (AFA 2010a; PJUCS 1994).

While the AFA is responsible for sustainable forest management in Algonquin Provincial Park (AFA 2010b), its governing legislation clearly intends for the Authority to maintain a commercial orientation, and it is a business owned by the provincial government. The AFA's primary responsibility is to manage tree harvesting and wood supply in the park to as many as 15 companies. Like other industry license holders, AFA's license must be approved by the Ontario Minister of Natural Resources, and operations must adhere to the provincial forest policy framework (i.e. the *Crown Forest Sustainability Act*). Moreover, in line with its special purpose, the community forest must also operate in conformance with the Algonquin Park Master Plan.

As an Ontario Crown agency, the government appoints the board of directors accountable to the Ontario Minister of Natural Resources and subject to ministerial discretion. As such, the board is not volunteer-driven, and members are compensated financially. Various interests are represented, but AFA is not technically considered a partnership model (e.g. community forest) in so far as board members are appointed based on their background rather than the goal of achieving formal representation for local communities or communities of interest (PJUCS 1994). Like other major licenses, AFA has a Local Citizens Committee and provides regular opportunities for public input (e.g. workshops, open houses).

Conversely, unlike other major licenses AFA does not pay full stumpage fees (resource rents) to the Crown, retaining about 90% of the stumpage generated. Instead this revenue goes "directly into local forest management, rather than to the Ontario treasury, [which] is a net benefit to the region, though possibly not to the province" (PJUCS 1994: 132). While difficult to measure, there are social benefits that accrue both locally and regionally as well as protection of intangible values and/or cultural ecosystem services demanded from Ontario's quintessential park. These social benefits are a result of proactively addressing potential conflict over park management and logging practices through a collaborative approach to environmental resource governance.

The park is 765,000 hectares (about 1,890,000 acres) and is located roughly 250 km from major population centers in southern Ontario (e.g. Toronto, Ottawa, Hamilton). Harvesting only occurs in the recreation–utilization zone, or about 481,000 hectares (about 1,190,000 acres), and less than 60% of that total area is available for forest harvesting. In terms of day-to-day operations, the park has a general manager who is accountable to the board, and a regular staff of about 23 with up to 15 additional seasonal staff. The organization is supported primarily by timber sales and receives some funding for silviculture (PJUCS 1994).

Logging remains controversial in Canada's oldest provincial park even though AFA primarily practices selection harvesting (i.e. <5% clear-cut) that is recognized by environmental groups (AFA 2010b). Given the publically sensitive operating area, non-industry stakeholders generally feel that logging levels are too high and directed by industry needs. For example, as part of ongoing efforts to reduce logging in the park, a coalition of environmental groups (Earthroots, Wildlands League, Forest Ethics, Greenpeace and Ontario Nature) retained Ecojustice (formerly Sierra Legal Defence Fund) early in the winter of 2009 to appeal the Canadian Standards Association Sustainable Forest Management certification of AFA operations (Earthroots 2009). Indeed, some in the industry acknowledge that without the creation of the AFA, there would not be a socially viable Algonquin-based forest industry (PJUCS 1994).

In terms of governance challenges, there has been some discord concerning the balance and selection of individuals on the AFA board and a preference for ensuring stronger "environmental" representation in keeping with the "park" status (PJUCS 1994). Accountability has been questioned in light of the fact that AFA, as a commercial corporation, does not hold public board meetings. Much like municipally controlled community forests in Ontario and British Columbia, having appointed rather than elected board members also brings into question the adequacy and legitimacy of representation (Beckley 1998; Bullock 2007). Within AFA's planning timetable, management plans are developed with community and interest groups through information sessions and public meetings (PJUCS 1994); however, the level of participation has recently been called into question (Earthroots 2009). In the past, AFA has also admitted that public information and education programs have not in fact been its strengths (PJUCS 1994).

Wendaban Stewardship Authority, 1990–1995

Motivation for creating the Wendaban Stewardship Authority (WSA) in Temagami, Ontario ramped up in 1988 when Minister of Natural Resources Vince Kerrio announced plans to commence logging road construction to access old-growth red and white pine in *n'Daki Menan* (our land), the traditional territory and ancestral home of the Teme-Augama Anishnabai (TAA) (Benidickson 1995; Shute and Knight 1995; TAA 2009). At the time the Teme-Augama Anishnabai had yet to settle a land claim for the region, asserting they had never signed treaties with the Crown, and there had been years of conflict involving indigenous, recreation and resource extraction groups. Environmental organizations, such as Temagami Wilderness Society, Wildlands League and Federation of Ontario Naturalists, were also concerned about potential logging in an interior area of the Temagami forest, which was adjacent to the recently created Lady Evelyn–Smoothwater Wilderness Provincial Park (Benidickson 1995). Pressure soon mounted from Aboriginal and non-Aboriginal logging road blockades, court actions taken by both Teme-Augama Anishnabai and environmental organizations, and international exposure.

On April 23, 1990 the provincial government, under then Liberal Premier David Peterson, and the Teme-Augama Anishnabai signed a Memorandum of Understanding (MOU) agreeing to create a joint stewardship council. As part of a larger settlement process, the WSA would assume responsibility for four townships and existing timber licenses at the heart of the long-simmering controversy (Benidickson 1995). As part of the MOU, Teme-Augama Anishnabai and Ontario agreed to enter a "treaty of co-existence" to resolve underlying points of conflict. Teme-Augama Anishnabai came forward with a proposal early in 1992 which set out three principles: stewardship throughout the region to ensure all life forms are sustained; the preservation of Aboriginal rights as inalienable rights that cannot be renounced; and ongoing co-existence and sharing of the land and resources to uphold stewardship and sustain life. The proposal included sole and shared stewardship zones whereby Teme-Augama Anishnabai and other public groups would share decision-making on some areas, while Teme-Augama Anishnabai and the province would have primary responsibility in others (Benidickson 1995). First Nations decision-making, governance structures and regulatory regimes would prevail in sole stewardship areas. However, Teme-Augama Anishnabai also acknowledged that some provincial and federal legislation might affect their management practices and that other communities could become involved in governance of sole stewardship areas. This proposal laid out the basic model for the WSA, which was established through a 1991 addendum to the 1990 MOU (PJUCS 1994).

A newly elected New Democratic Party government quickly responded to the proposal and outlined its own prescriptions for the governance model. The Authority would have to represent Aboriginal and non-Aboriginal local residents and be responsive to citizens' interests in other parts of the province. The mandate would be flexible to enable natural resource development as well as conservation of ecosystems, biodiversity, and recreational opportunities. During the summer of 1993, the province and Teme-Augama Anishnabai agreed that a shared stewardship body would control nearly 1,300 km² of unpatented Crown land centering on Lake Temagami, which included wilderness and waterway parks. Given the complexity of the issues and negotiations at hand, the agreement passed but was met with resistance from local Aboriginal and non-Aboriginal groups for various reasons (Benidickson 1995).

Teme-Augama Anishnabai and the Ontario government intended to "assign responsibility to the WSA to plan, decide, implement, enforce, regulate, and monitor all uses of and activities on the land within its area of jurisdiction" (Benidickson 1995). As Benidickson (1995: 5) points out, "this was a notable expansion of the authority over timber licenses originally conferred by the MOU." To fulfill its mandate, WSA would undertake adaptive management through monitoring, studying and planning land uses and activities on the land (Benidickson 1995). All findings would be reported to the province and to Teme-Augama Anishnabai.

The board had 12 members including one-third Teme-Augama Anishnabai and two-thirds provincial appointees (with a 1-year renewable term), plus a mutually agreed upon chairperson.[1] Provincial appointees included, for example, individuals from the forest industry (1), labor (1), environmental (1), recreation and tourism (1), community development (1) and the Township of Temagami (1) (Dust 1995; Matakala 1995). It is noteworthy that OMNR was not represented (Matakala 1995). Decisions would be made by consensus based on a 75% majority. Like the AFA, any revenues generated from existing and future permits, licenses and leases under WSA jurisdiction would return to the management body, subject to provincial taxes (Dust 1995).

Between 1993 and 1995, WSA worked to develop a 20-year stewardship plan (1994–2014). The plan embraced an ecosystem-based management approach designed to operationalize the Brundtland Commission definition of sustainable development (Benidickson 1995). Guidelines were established for fish and wildlife, wetlands, recreation and tourism, cottage and commercial development, and timber production (Dust 1995). The plan also included specific guidelines for "cultural and heritage trails, portages, campsites, village sites and other significant places, including archeological or spiritual ones" (Laronde 1993: 98). Old-growth pine was to be permanently protected. Locals and soft-touch logging and hauling operators would be given priority when awarding cutting licenses.

Despite its potential, the Authority encountered sizable barriers. According to Teme-Augama Anishnabai, "The Authority completed their Land Use Plan but had no funding or workers to implement it" (TAA 2009), suggesting a lack of resources during a formative operational development stage. As we noted in Chapter 2, implementation is affected by many factors. The 1997 Royal Commission of Aboriginal People also found that WSA was hamstrung by the failed provincial promise of legislative jurisdiction over the four townships. Without a clear legislative base WSA's decisions "were challenged by district staff of the Ministry of Natural Resources" (RCAP 1997). Matakala (1995: 67) also found that WSA lacked the authority to act on its own decisions, and that WSA had continually tried to get the province to broaden the WSA mandate through some form of ownership or legislative jurisdiction akin to the AFA's arrangement. The fact that WSA did not have OMNR representation on its board was probably a strategic move to maximize local decision-making control, but may have been ill-advised in the long run.

While legislation to empower the WSA had been introduced in Cabinet by August 17, 1992 (Matakala 1995), the Authority began to wind down in February 1995. By June 1995, that legislation still had not been passed when Conservative Premier Mike Harris was elected, which ensured a new political tack. The WSA was replaced with an advisory board – the Temagami Comprehensive Planning Council (CPC) – intended to steer plan development and manage consultation for the Temagami district as a whole (some 66 townships or 717,400 ha) (PJUCS 1994; Benidickson 1995). Since 1991, the Council has been enlarged to include Aboriginal representation and a co-chair through the 1993 addendum to the MOU that had also established the WSA. First Nations had long refused to participate on the Council, stating it was premature given the unsettled status of the Treaty of Co-existence (PJUCS 1994). Past interviews with CPC participants suggest that OMNR might have preferred to manage Temagami's issues and planning through a single consultation process and board that was ultimately accountable to OMNR's Temagami District Manager. A report commissioned by the OMNR (PJUCS 1994: 143) concluded, "the belief that CPC is no more than a front for OMNR or a device for legitimizing OMNR decisions (but at the same time an excuse for OMNR to avoid decisions) is apparently fairly widely held."

While ephemeral, WSA contributed to strengthening personal relationships and awareness and learning through providing a face-to-face forum for direct and thorough discussion. WSA members thought that their model helped to negate needless misunderstandings firing conflict among social groups and that the process generated a management plan with broad local support (though one that would not necessarily please OMNR) (Laronde 1993; Dust 1995). Regardless of the outcome, First Nations leadership considered the WSA process itself to be a "tremendous success" in terms of how conflict was mitigated through consensus building (Laronde 1993: 101).

Ontario Community Forest Pilot Program, 1991–1994

Ontario's Community Forest Pilot Program represented the first meaningful provincial experiment with establishing community forests on Crown lands in the industrial resource hinterland of northern Ontario. Troubles commonly associated with "underserved" forest resource-dependent towns (see Bagby and Kusel 2003), namely their disproportionately low benefits versus high impacts from resource development, were brought to the forefront by the Ontario Royal Commission on the Northern Environment (1985) and Committee on Resource Dependent Communities in Northern Ontario (1986) (Harvey and Hillier 1994: 726).

When the New Democratic Party formed a new government in 1990 it immediately directed OMNR to implement community forests. The expressed intent was to "provide greater opportunity for community involvement in all aspects of forest management" (Harvey and Hillier 1994: 725).

In January 1991, the Lakehead University Forestry Association held its 23rd annual symposium, choosing community forestry as a timely theme. Speaking to a crowd of over 200 foresters, students, professionals and tradespeople from northern Ontario, NDP Minister of Natural Resources, the Hon. Bud Wildman, discussed provincial policy and future plans concerning community forestry (Wildman 1990, in Smith and Whitmore 1990). Minister Wildman heralded the AFA as an earlier example of a provincially supported community forest in Ontario and endorsed the model as one that could work to advance sustainable forest management by communities in northern Ontario in particular. The minister based his support on the perceived high level of meaningful local involvement in decision-making achieved by the AFA. The minister also openly acknowledged that a single model would not function across geographical contexts.[2]

Staff from OMNR conducted preliminary policy research and determined that a limited number of 4-year pilot sites should be established (Harvey and Hillier 1994). Subsequently, the formal announcement for the Community Forest Pilot Program came in March 1991. The approach was to create a practical experiment to examine the opportunities for increasing community involvement in forestry. As evinced by high-profile conflicts in northeastern Ontario (notably at Temagami) and community forest advocacy workshops in the northwest (e.g. the 1991 Lakehead University Forestry Association Symposium on Community Forestry), there was strong interest at the community level in gaining more control over local resources and decisions. At the time there were no legislated citizen advisory committees in the planning process for industrial forest management. During the late summer and fall of 1991, OMNR arranged a series of newspaper advertisements and information sessions, as well as discussions with communities, to inform communities and solicit statements of interest. In keeping with the experimental nature of the project, the government then invited "any coalition of local constituents with an interest in a common forest" to come forward. In all, 22 statements of interests were received (Harvey and Hillier 1994).

Following review, four successful sites were announced in March 1992. These were the Town of Geraldton; the Wikwemikong First

Nation; the Town of Elk Lake; and the 6/70 Area Economic Diversification Committee in the Kapuskasing area (Harvey 1995). The pilot community forests were created and provisions for delegating power were later put in the Crown Forest Sustainability Act (1994, c.25, s.15(1)): "The Minister may establish forest management boards for such areas as are designated by the Minister, including forest management boards for community forests designated by the Minister." Like the AFA, the pilots were to operate within the larger provincial framework, regulation and policies, and each pilot had to respect existing resource commitments on the land (tourism, fiber allocations). While the pilots would have a designated Crown land base, tenure was not granted and stayed with existing tenure holders (Harvey 1995). All resource management projects were subject to OMNR approval, which retained final authority and responsibility for resources management planning and program delivery under the Crown Forest Sustainability Act.

From the provincial perspective, the pilot project aimed to implement "sustainable forestry" that would integrate social, economic and ecological considerations: namely, forestry practices that would support community development, promotion of resource stewardship, and management of forest user conflicts locally, rather than having conflicts escalate to the provincial level (Harvey and Hillier 1994). To maintain flexibility and be responsive to local contexts, OMNR encouraged pilot sites to design their community forests in alignment with local desires and needs. For example, the size of each community forest was different (Wikwemikong, 42,600 ha; Geraldton, 65,000 ha; 6/70 Area, 333,000 ha; Elk Lake, 470,000 ha). Accordingly, Geraldton focused on remedial silviculture and ecosystem-based management approaches (Harvey and Hillier 1994); Elk Lake focused on management planning and information gathering; 6/70 Area Economic Diversification Committee was mandated to coordinate community economic development and focused on empowerment and amplifying the community voice in resource management, public awareness and conflict resolution. Wikwemikong First Nation supported a holistic approach to diversifying and promoting natural resource harvest, use, regeneration and marketing with an eye to creating opportunity and quality of life. As a First Nation community, all forest resource management activities were to be determined based on benefits to all band members, the environment and "the culture and tradition of Wikwemikong."

Different governance models were encouraged to accommodate varying social and economic contexts and to broaden lessons learned from the "experiment." Elk Lake included a single community and adopted a partnership committee model with appointed members to represent prominent local groups (e.g. labor, First Nation, recreation users, environmentalists, local business and government, education and OMNR). The 6/70 site also selected a board of directors to represent significant groups, including individuals from six partner communities. In contrast, Geraldton formed a non-profit corporation which reserved steering committee seats for representatives from the town, OMNR and forest industry (i.e. Kimberly-Clark) as well as six formally elected at-large representatives drawn from residents of participating townships (Harvey 1995). Located on Unceded Indian Reserve #26, Wikwemikong First Nation was a network of six communities with one council. Council assigned responsibility to the Wikwemikong Development Commission, to be guided by the band's Land and Resource Committee. The OMNR sat on steering committees for the three mainly non-Aboriginal pilots, and met with Wikwemikong Development Commission staff as required for technical support and updates, in keeping with the government-to-government relationship between Ontario and the First Nation. There is a parallel here to the Temagami case whereby First Nations-led models rarely want OMNR involved in decision-making.

The OMNR granted up to $100,000 Canadian dollars (CAD) to supplement community contributions ($50,000) in order to set up the organization, hire staff, bring in consultants, arrange public consultation and develop a management plan. Subsequently, another $100,000 CAD was provided for information gathering to support plan development. Later project implementation funding ranged from $160,000 to $420,000 CAD (Harvey 1995). Additional external funding flowed in from other government programs, business and community clubs, and many sites drew on in-kind contributions of time and expertise. Once established, the pilots were expected to undertake projects on a cost recovery basis save for non-revenue-producing work conducted in the best interests of the province. The goal of short-term self-sufficiency (within one and a half to two years of operation) turned out to be overambitious and was not realized. The province later deemed this a major lesson – the ephemeral start-up period set by the province was "not long enough to determine whether a new community forest partnership is close to achieving self-sufficiency" (Harvey 1995: 16).

After showing great promise, Ontario's Community Forest Pilot Program was scrapped in 1994. None of the pilots were granted tenure over their assigned Crown land base. Perhaps the ambitious short-term goal of self-sufficiency was in part designed to give emerging community organizations a chance to resist such a political fate. Only Wikwemikong First Nation persisted in a meaningful way as a community forest because they had a secure land base (Teitelbaum *et al.* 2006). Both Elk Lake and Geraldton morphed into forest management consulting, servicing and contracting businesses serving existing forest companies and forest stakeholders and essentially began competing with other small business ventures in the northern forest sector. The 6/70 coalition quickly dissolved with the termination of funding and provincial-assigned authority.

Some key challenges for the pilots were encountered in working to build awareness and support for their models and maintaining collaboration. For example, 6/70 found it difficult to persuade the six towns spread along 70 miles (113 km) of highway to work together, "particularly when there [was] no pressing cause to rally together" (Harvey 1995: 49). Apparently, the absence of hot button issues – whether environmental, First Nations rights, economic or otherwise – created confusion among community members regarding the need for the community forest (Harvey 1995: 50). Consequently, 6/70 also struggled with meeting attendance. Conversely, reaching band consensus on a forest policy to guide and regulate timber harvest of a community forest commons was a particular challenge for Wikwemikong First Nation (Harvey and Hillier 1994: 728). First Nations engagement was an ongoing challenge for the Elk Lake Community Forest; First Nations had never participated despite having dedicated seats on the board.

The biggest challenge for the non-Aboriginal community pilots proved to be the lack of forest tenure and therefore meaningful authority over forest resources. Ambiguity surrounding their authority and responsibilities led Elk Lake into jurisdictional conflicts with two OMNR district offices and Temagami's Comprehensive Planning Council (discussed above) (Harvey 1995). As observed by 6/70, having no legislated authority created conflict among its partners regarding appropriate types and levels of project involvement. For the 6/70 coalition, part of the problem was that the committee chair was from the dominant forest industry group, which clearly contributed to a power imbalance (if not a conflict of interest) at the board level. Moreover, 6/70's economic development role in resource development created turf problems with several other local groups involved in economic development initiatives in the area. In other instances, Geraldton found it needed a commitment of some sort with its major license holder (Kimberly-Clark) and/or OMNR to enable community forest harvesting and silviculture. It was unreasonable that the local organization had to get written permission from organized labor (representing forest workers linked to the major license holder), an agreement with the company and a cutting license from OMNR for each harvesting-related project. Such hindrances also restricted investment by Geraldton Community Forest and local entrepreneurs (Harvey 1995).

Westwind Stewardship Incorporated, 1996 to present

As the Ontario Pilot Program was being phased out, a similar experiment in local stakeholder involvement was taking form elsewhere in cottage country. Westwind Stewardship Inc. (WSI) was initiated based on ideas from local government staff who, during a period of tenure restructuring, recognized an opportunity to do things differently (Clark *et al.* 2003). And much like AFA, a primary driver for Westwind was the perceived high potential for conflict over industrial forestry in Ontario's prime cottage country – the areas of Muskoka and Parry Sound, which are bounded by Georgian Bay to the west, Algonquin Park to the east and larger urban centers of southern Ontario to the south. Unlike the community forest pilot projects, however, the plan was to have Westwind take control of an entire Sustainable Forest License that had been previously managed by industry (similar to AFA and to what TAA might have been had it been allowed to advance).

Discussions with Local Citizen Committee members led to the appointment of a transition team during fall 1996. The transition team "sought to create a company that was independent of direct influence by forest products companies" (Clark *et al.* 2003). Then in December 1996 a letter of intent was submitted to provincial government that stated the transition team's aim of negotiating a Sustainable Forest License. Westwind was incorporated in April 1997 and signed a license agreement in May 1998, securing Ivey Foundation funding one month later. Full takeover of management planning was set for 2002, and forest certification was approved in February 2002 (WSI 2005).

As a Sustainable Forest License holder, Westwind is subject to the same policies and legislation as industrial license holders that manage for timber extraction (Crown Forest Sustainability Act 1996). However, its stated objectives seek ecologically sustainable forest management on a diverse and intensively used forest land base. Westwind "will serve forest businesses and other users of the forest while maintaining the highest standards for business practice and public accountability" (WSI 2005). As with other Sustainable Forest License holders, its responsibilities include planning timber harvest; planting; monitoring; public reporting; preparation of Forest Management Plans; and self-regulation of forest operations in accordance with government guidelines. Above and beyond its legal responsibilities, Westwind is committed to training and education.

A major difference from other Sustainable Forest License holders is that Westwind was designed to position a collection of local social groups as managers of public lands by agreement with the province (i.e. through a Sustainable Forest License). The license includes the Municipalities of the District of Muskoka and District of Parry Sound as well as the County of Haliburton, which together include towns such as Bracebridge, Huntsville, Parry Sound and Gravenhurst, as well as numerous small towns and six First Nations (Clark *et al.* 2003; WSI 2005). The community-based, non-profit corporation includes a consensus-based board of seven community and industry members, which notably comprises four at-large community members, one large industry member, one middle-sized mill member and one independent forestry contractor. The Westwind board is chaired by one of the at-large community members (Clark *et al.* 2003).

Operationally, the organization has a staff of seven and manages an area-based tenure for 360,000 ha of public land in the French Severn forest. Main funding comes from the forest industry (e.g. Forest Renewal Fund and Forest Futures) (Durocher 2008), but funding can come from other private sources such as the Richard Ivey Foundation when funds are used to undertake projects for sustainability and ecosystem biodiversity (WSI 2005). Its annual operating budget of about 1.4 million (2008) is heavily supported by timber dollars. Monies from a "partnerships" budget pay for training and education, Forest Sustainability Council certification and periodic conferences. Westwind's main clients have been Tembec and Domtar (Clark *et al.* 2003).

Berry (2006) outlines four main benefits of the Westwind model. As non-profit, the organization does not have to meet shareholders' expectations (presumably maximization of financial profit) but can address an array of local values. Through a demonstrated track record, Westwind has also proved that non-profit management of public land can be successful (as in Creston, BC, Chapter 5). Berry (2006) also sees Forest Stewardship Council (FSC) certification as an indication that Westwind carries out ecologically, socially and economically sustainable practices and as evidence of public confidence in the operation. Westwind's ability to attract private dollars also makes it self-sufficient, avoiding dependence on government subsidies (unlike the pilot projects, agreement forests and formerly Conservation Authorities).

Admittedly, "moving from discussion to implementation was slow and fraught with misgivings" (Clark *et al.* 2003) and some limitations continue to dog the organization. Given its small staff and resources, the board and staff must be very entrepreneurial. While a strategic plan was developed early and many objectives have been accomplished, in the past Westwind has had difficulty systematically updating this plan, because of capacity limitations. As well, a First Nations advisory group provides some input, but efforts to expand the board to fully include First Nations have yet to be realized (Clark *et al.* 2003).

SUCCESSES AND CHALLENGES WITH COMMUNITY FORESTRY
IN ONTARIO

The Ontario experience indicates a relatively long and successful record of experimenting with community forestry. While some models failed outright or fell prey to changing provincial leadership and OMNR policy (e.g. the pilots and Wendaban), others were scaled back (Agreement Forests) and refocused for current issues (Conservation Authorities) once they had outlived their original mandates. Others remain experiments – particularly those in cottage country and parks (Westwind, AFA) – and have maintained a "business as usual" mode so long as they have worked to contain conflict and pacify calls for radical reforms of forest governance.

In general, each of the above cases owes its creation to actual or potential social conflicts arising from tensions between conservation and development interests. In the provincial south, where private land ownership is high (owned by mainly individuals or lower-level governments), provincial policy to support and even lead active community-based management efforts were a welcomed and effective response to significant problems of economy and environment created by the poor land management practices of the day. Yet the ongoing failure of provincial policy to remedy the structural problems of northern Crown forest governance and economy, namely issues of proprietary control and use of public and Aboriginal forest lands, has maintained a political and economic climate ripe for periodic upheaval, reactive policy tinkering and experimentation with community forestry. As industrial forest interests have historically prevailed in northern Ontario, it is not surprising that the community forest option has been reserved as a one-off solution for socially inoperable settings where competing land uses and visions have not been easily reconciled by conventional top-down processes.

As shown in the above cases, community forestry in Ontario has tended to endure at times when and in regions where the provincial government has followed through with community forest programs, policies and, most significantly, legislation (i.e. Agreements, Conservation Authorities, Algonquin Forest Authority). For instance, the three non-Aboriginal community forest pilot project sites as well as Wendaban had no formal authority. This in turn created jurisdictional problems and confusion among stakeholders and opponents (e.g. industry, district level OMNR, local economic development, neighboring public participation processes) involved in the sites and/or in other endeavors intended to address the same or similar problems. Moreover, since WSA and the three pilots were never granted tenure nor recognized by powerful actors as accepted practice, they were easily defeated.

Not without their challenges, AFA and Westwind continue to operate as large-scale license holders, but they do so in contexts where board members and affluent seasonal residents and tourists expect limitations on development. The AFA and Westwind have been able to sate existing industry interests and appease cottagers, local politicians and environmental organizations. Agreement Forests and Conservation Authorities primarily operate on southern private lands and for conservation purposes, negating many of the social and political problems associated with industrial resource extraction and Crown land.

Lessons from experience

Ontario's community forestry experience has generated several operational lessons. The above experiences provide insights on the accomplishments of small collaborative organizations operating in uneven policy networks, growing recognition for cross-cultural sensitivities, and the development of participatory and management capacity (i.e. skills, organizational and communication networks, social capital, physical resources) in hinterland regions (see Laronde 1993; Harvey and Hillier 1994; PJUCS 1994; Harvey 1995). Based on two decades of organizational performance, we also now know that when emerging community forest organizations do not secure meaningful authority over a land base, they evolve away from aspirations of local decision-making in forest governance. Instead they change into locally competitive contracting, consulting and servicing arrangements that service the existing industry and government. This captures the local knowledge and skills, trained personnel and resources that community forest organizations would otherwise use if they themselves were directing and undertaking planning and management in their own designated forests and communities (e.g. Geraldton, Elk Lake). In fact this has been a growing trend in both Canada and the United States over about the past decade. The backfilling of service needs may distract community forestry organizations from achieving their mandate, but it also points out the limitations of government and business while demonstrating that local capacity and social capital exist (Bullock 2007; Danks 2008).

One after another, multi-party community-based collaborations have encountered a general reluctance to decentralize control over public forests. One reason is that the conventional forest industry remains a "sacred cow" fiercely guarded by a state-controlled system of forestry science and management administered by professionally trained and specialized techno-bureaucrats with vested interests (Robson 2010). A First Nations leader involved in the Wendaban Stewardship Authority process reflected on this challenge and offered a prognosis:

> Can MNR become an agent for the public, for the people of Ontario? Or is it always going to be in control? That is a major issue. When you have this kind of entrenchment in both thought and power, in process, in thinking and in how things are done, the initial response is that the status quo must be maintained. I guess that we are looking at systemic change – a "paradigm" shift. (Laronde 1993: 101–2)

Furthermore, in many forest-dependent towns a strong interest-based community links the livelihoods, lifestyles and traditions of forest workers and their families (and local businesses for that matter) to forestry professionals in the local mills and OMNR offices (and their families). This social arrangement is characterized by a paternal company–town relationship and local culture of resource dependence (Reed 1990; Bullock, in press).

Another reason for resistance is that community forestry concepts and practices in Ontario (and indeed Canada) are not clearly theorized, well-documented, tested and widely accepted. There seems to be an implicit fear of the unknown manifest in community forestry literature, even in the most up-to-date dialogues. This undermines critical and constructive advocacy that could actually sway detractors who otherwise can conveniently continue to cite the common caveats of idealism and panacea in community forestry discourse. There remains a scarcity of research and information on community forestry in Ontario, and no coordinating structure exists to identify, assemble and organize that which does exist for ready access.

In the absence of open and insightful debate on the possibilities of community forestry and tenure reform in Ontario, uncertainty continues to create doubt among community forestry supporters and critics alike. However, owing to the unprecedented decade-on forestry crisis in Ontario, numerous additional civil society, Aboriginal and academic groups have emerged to address these issues, examples being the Northern Ontario Sustainable Communities Partnership (NOSCP); Saving the Region of Ontario North Group (STRONG); Common Voice Initiative; Northeast Superior Regional Chiefs' Forum; Northeast Superior Forest Community (NSFC); Whitefeather Forest Initiative (Pikangikum First Nation); Gorden Cosens Survival Group; Institute for Northern Ontario Research and Development (INORD). Indeed, tenure reform and community forests in Ontario became hot topics at several workshops and conferences in recent years. For example, the 52nd and 53rd annual meetings of the Ontario Professional Foresters Association featured local control through tenure reform and community forests, respectively, in 2009 and 2010. Lakehead University (2009 and 2011), University of Toronto (2010) and Algoma University (2011) all hosted public workshops. At these events, invited speakers from provincial ministries, First Nations, resource communities, academics, industry and environmental groups addressed hundreds of delegates to discuss tenure reform and community forestry.

Community forests have become a somewhat taboo topic among forestry practitioners and politicians because the concept and practice have not been fully explained or understood, and local control has been perceived as a threat to the status quo (Bullock *et al.* 2012). As Clark *et al.* (2003) point out, "The concept of a different approach to tenure for [large-scale industrial forest licenses] has frequently been discussed and rarely written about, at least publicly." Repeated characterizations using terms such as "small-scale," "pilot," "project" or "experiment" only serve to reinforce the idea that community forests are novel, naïve and/or peripheral concepts for policy makers and managers to entertain while handling bigger forestry clients and problems.

But by all accounts, the excuse that community forestry is unproven does not provide sufficient rationale for its premature defeat. As Robinson (2008) points out:

> The dominant [forestry] model, has clearly failed in several important ways, but existing community forest experiments are, at best, very preliminary prototypes ... There can be no experimental test of the relative merits of the two systems because there are simply no community forests that can be rigorously compared to the mature corporate and

administrative structures. In the absence of empirical evidence decisions will be made on political and theoretical grounds.

That community forestry has continued to struggle in Ontario is not for a lack of local capacity, in-province or home-grown attempts to provide blueprints,[3] or experience with different forms of local control. What has been lacking is a provincial vision, commitment and a systematic approach to implementing operational community forests that are backed by well-developed policy and legislation, industry support, and integrated local and technical knowledge on social and ecological elements of forest systems.

NOTES

1 The implemented board structure differed from the original Teme-Augama Anishnabai proposal to have 50/50 TAA–Ontario representation (see Benidickson 1995). This arrangement was maintained in spite of opposition from First Nation participants who initially wanted a kind of regional governance including 50/50 arrangement between First Nations and local residents to strengthen local control relative to that of the OMNR (Dust 1995).

2 Almost 20 years after Wildman's comments, on April 23, 2009, Ontario Minister of Natural Resources, Donna Cansfield (Liberal), announced to delegates at the Ontario Professional Foresters Association annual meeting in Sudbury, Ontario that a formal review of Ontario's Crown tenure system would commence. Provincial officials again indicated provincial interest in the AFA and recognized the need for context specific management models to handle contextual diversity in Ontario.

3 Auden pioneered a vision for a "Forest Village" in Nipigon, northern Ontario in *The Forestry Chronicle* in 1944, providing full details for a cooperative community forest and integrated planning and management more than 65 years ago (Auden 1944).

REFERENCES

Algonquin Forestry Authority (AFA) (2010a). *Annual Report.* Pembroke and Huntsville, ON: AFA.

Algonquin Forestry Authority (AFA) (2010b). Algonquin Forestry Authority homepage. Available at http://www.algonquinforestry.on.ca/. Accessed October 30, 2010.

Armson, K. (2001). *Ontario Forests: A Historical Perspective*, Ontario: Fitzhenry and Whiteside Ltd. and Ontario Forestry Association.

Auden, A. (1944). Nipigon forest village. *Forestry Chronicle* 20(4): 209–61.

Bagby, K. and Kusel, J. (2003). *Civic Science Partnerships in Community Forestry: Building Capacity for Participation among Underserved Communities.* Taylorsville, CA: Forest Community Research.

Beckley, T. (1998). Moving toward consensus-based forest management: A comparison of industrial, co-managed, community and small private forests in Canada. *Forestry Chronicle* 74(5): 736–44.

Benidickson, J. (1995). Temagami old growth: Pine, politics, and public policy. *Environments* **23**(2): 41–50.

Berry, A. (2006). *Branching Out: Case Studies in Canadian Forest Management.* Bozeman, MT: Property and Environment Research Centre.

Bullock, R. (2007). Two sides of the forest. *Journal of Soil and Water Conservation* **62**(1): 12A–15A.

Bullock, R. (in press).'Mill town' identity crisis: Reframing community and the culture of forest resource dependence in single industry towns. In Parkins, J. and Reed, M. (eds.), *Social Transformation in Rural Canada: New Insights into Community, Cultures, and Collective Action.* Vancouver, BC, UBC Press.

Bullock, R., Armitage, D. and Mitchell, B. (2012). Shadow networks, social learning and collaborating through crisis: Building resilient forest-based communities in Northern Ontario, Canada. In Goldstein, B. (ed.), *Collaborative Resilience: Moving through Crisis to Opportunity.* MIT Press, 309–37.

Clark, T., Harvey, S., Bruemmer, G. and Walker, J. (2003). *Large-scale Community Forestry in Ontario, Canada: A Sign of the Times.* Paper submitted to the XII World Forestry Congress, 2003, Quebec City.

Danks, C. (2008). Institutional arrangements in community-based forestry. In Donoghue, E. and Sturtevant, V. (eds.), *Forest Community Connections: Implications for Research, Management, and Governance.* Washington: Resources for the Future, pp.185–204.

Durocher, C. (2008). *Westwind Forest Stewardship Inc. Financial Statements.* March 31, 2008. Parry Sound, ON: Westwind Forest Stewardship Inc.

Dust, T. (1995). *The Impact of Aboriginal Land Claims and Self-Government on Canadian municipalities: The Local Government Perspective.* Toronto: ICURR Press.

Earthroots (2009). Environmental organizations band together to appeal Algonquin sustainable forest certification. Available at http://earthroots.org. Accessed December 9, 2010.

Harvey, S. (1995). *Ontario Community Forest Pilot Project: Lessons Learned 1991–1994. Taking Stock of Ontario's Community Forestry Experience.* Sault Ste Marie: Queen's Printer for Ontario.

Harvey, S. and Hillier, B. (1994). Community forestry in Ontario. *Forestry Chronicle* **70**: 725–30.

Laronde, M. (1993). Co-management of lands and resources in n'Daki Menan. In Mawhiney, A. (ed.), *Rebirth: Political, Economic, and Social Development in First Nations.* Toronto, ON: Dundurn Press, pp. 93–106.

Matakala, P. (1995). Decision-making and conflict resolution in co-management: Two cases from Temagami, Northeastern Ontario. Unpublished doctoral dissertation. Lakehead University, Thunder Bay, Ontario.

Ontario Ministry of Natural Resources (OMNR) (1986). *Evergreen Challenge: The Agreement Forest Story.* Toronto, ON: Queen's Printer for Ontario.

Ontario Ministry of Natural Resources (OMNR) (1987). *A Review of the Conservation Authorities Program.* Toronto, ON: OMNR.

Ontario Ministry of Community and Social Services (OMCSS) (2008). Info notes: Aboriginal population. *Info Notes* 6, March 2008.

P.J. Usher Consulting Services (PJUCS) (1994). *Partnerships for Community Involvement in Forestry: A Comparative Analysis of Community Involvement in Natural Resource Management.* Sault Ste Marie: Ontario Ministry of Natural Resources.

Reed, M. (1990). Managing for sustainable development: A case study of a hinterland community, Ignace, Ontario, Canada. Unpublished doctoral dissertation. Waterloo, ON: Department of Geography, University of Waterloo, Ontario.

Royal Commission on Aboriginal Peoples (RCAP) (1997). *Report of the Royal Commission on Aboriginal Peoples* Ottawa, ON: Government of Canada.

Richardson, A. (1974). *Conservation by the People: The History of the Conservation Movement in Ontario to 1970.* Toronto, ON: University of Toronto Press.

Robinson, D. (2008). *The Science of Community Forests. Part 1: Approaching Regime Change Systematically.* INORD Working Paper 2–08.

Robson, M. (2010). Sustainable forestry in the 21st century: Multiple voices, multiple knowledges. *Forestry Chronicle* **86**(6): 667–8.

Shute, J. and Knight, D. (1995). Obtaining an understanding of environmental knowledge: Wendaban Stewardship Authority. *Canadian Geographer* **39**(2): 101–11.

Smith, P. and Whitmore, G. (1990). *Community Forestry: Proceedings of the Lakehead University Forestry Association 23rd Annual Symposium, January 25–26.* Occasional Paper 8. Centre for Northern Studies, Lakehead University.

Teitelbaum, S., Beckley, T. and Nadeau, S. (2006). A national portrait of community forestry on public land in Canada. *Forestry Chronicle* **82**(3): 416–28.

Teme-Augama Anishnabai (2009). Temagami First Nation homepage: TAA negotiations office. Available at http://www.temagamifirstnation.ca/. Accessed December 1, 2010.

Westwind Stewardship Inc. (WSI) (2005). Homepage. Available at http://www.westwindforest.ca. Accessed December 1, 2010.

Zavitz, E. (1909). *Fifty Years of Reforestation in Ontario.* Toronto, ON: Ontario Department of Lands and Forest.

5

A "watershed" case for community forestry in British Columbia's interior: the Creston Valley Forest Corporation

This chapter provides a case study of the early grassroots organizing and operational challenges in what has been widely regarded as a success story for community forestry. The reality is that Creston's community forest has had to struggle to maintain itself, remain viable and build local support. The story of the Creston Valley Forest Corporation (CVFC) provides the archetypical case of the promise and the implementation challenges associated with community forestry in a conflicted, multiple-use forest setting.

COMMUNITY CONTEXT, TOWN OF CRESTON,
BRITISH COLUMBIA

The community of Creston is located in the Kootenay region of British Columbia's interior, just north of the US border. The 8.5-km² town site lies in the scenic Kootenay River Valley, bounded by the Selkirk and Purcell Mountains. Incorporated as a municipality in 1924, the current population is 4,826 (Statistics Canada 2006). Creston is surrounded by a number of unincorporated communities and large tracts of Crown land within the Regional District of Central Kootenay (Creston 2005). The Lower Kootenay Indian Band (of Ktunaxa First Nation) has 25.5 km² of reserve land in the vicinity.

Mining was the main interest of the first European settlers who pushed north from the United States via the Dewdney Trail in the late 1800s (Creston 2001). But by the early 1900s, agriculture and forestry became the main drivers of the local economy. The first sawmill was built in the first decade of the 1900s, and fruit and grain agriculture became highly productive. As in the rest of British Columbia, Creston's forest economy is in transition. Notably, Crestbrook Forest Industries began scaling back operations in the early 1980s, closing its Creston mill in 1991 (Sunderman 2003). Wood processing operations were moved to nearby Cranbrook so that half of the wood harvested in the Creston area is now processed out of town. J. H. Huscroft Ltd. and Wyndell Box Ltd. are the largest lumber mills operating in the Creston area, consuming about 260,000 m^3 of wood annually (Creston 2004). These local mills now heavily depend upon private wood supplies because of regional wood shortages.

Manufacturing is important to the local economy, given the links to agriculture and forestry. In 2006, 205 people were employed in agriculture and other resource-based industries (primary sector), while another 270 people were in manufacturing and construction industries (Statistics Canada 2006). Community planning objectives focus on the expansion of value-added and secondary industries to "help ensure raw resources from the agricultural and forestry sectors, as well as other sectors, do not leave the Valley before processing has taken place" (Creston 2005: 8). The Columbia Brewing Company, the largest brewery in western Canada with annual beer sales of $440 million, also provides many jobs locally. Amenity migrants, mostly retirees and summer residents, have been slowly purchasing properties in and around Creston. The brewery, fruit industry and town water supply depend heavily on water from the pristine Arrow Creek watershed, an 8,500-ha (21,000-acre) watershed located 8 km (5 miles) northeast of the town on Crown land (Figure 5.1).

INTEGRATING COMMUNITY WATERSHED AND FOREST MANAGEMENT: THE EMERGENCE OF THE CRESTON VALLEY FOREST CORPORATION

The CVFC, based in Creston, British Columbia, was formed because of enduring pressure to harvest the Arrow Creek watershed (Figure 5.2). Since the 1970s, residents had fought to keep logging out of the watershed owing to potential impacts on water quality and quantity that could jeopardize domestic and industrial water supplies. The last harvesting in the watershed was some high-grade logging done by J. H. Huscroft during the early 1970s. With the exit of industry, local residents were adamant that Arrow Creek be preserved.

By the late 1970s the community was embroiled in a controversy over logging, wood shortages for the local mills, and forest industry claims that environmental constraints were limiting timber supplies around the town of Creston. In an attempt to mitigate conflict, British Columbia's Forest Minister came to Creston in April 1977 to introduce a

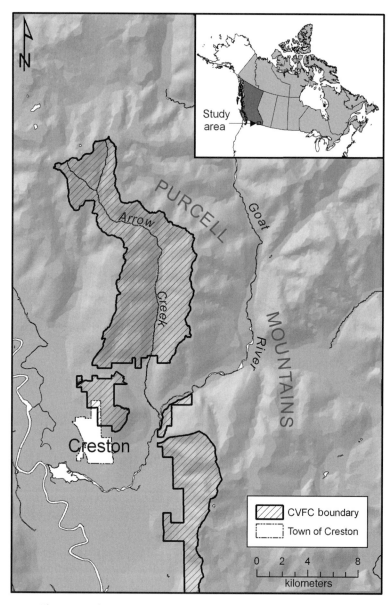

Figure 5.1 The controversial Creston Valley Forest Corporation operating area and Arrow Creek watershed, Creston, British Columbia (map created by J. A. Carnegie and R. Bullock).

new Public Advisory Committee (PAC). The first of its kind in British Columbia, the PAC was composed of community and industry representatives and would advise on the management of Crown lands around

Figure 5.2 Arrow Creek, Creston, British Columbia (photo: R. Bullock).

Creston. Coincidently, the local forester selected as the first PAC chairman would later become the first manager of the community forest in Creston.

The PAC was later dissolved in the early 1990s when the province introduced the Commission on Resource and the Environment (CORE), a large-scale, multi-stakeholder initiative for regional land-use planning implemented to classify the Crown land base. This process led to the Kootenay Boundary Land Use Plan being produced, but the town and pro-watershed protection interests in Creston failed to have Arrow Creek removed from the timber harvesting land base. A key stakeholder, the Erickson Improvement District – the board responsible for operating the water supply system since the 1920s – had strategically refused to participate in the planning process. In hindsight, this may have been a poor decision.

By 1991, Crestbrook Forest Industries had closed its Creston plant and was shipping nearly half of the wood harvested in the Creston area to Cranbrook for processing (Sunderman 2003). In response, residents formed a lobby group to express concern for the loss of wood supply and to explore local opportunities for wood manufacturing and local economic development. Participants were both environmentally and economically minded but shared a common vision of increased forest-derived benefits for their community. As a provincial timber review had found a surplus of unallocated timber in the area, local lobbying persuaded government to offer a community-held tenure to permit local control of watershed management. By 1996, the local Member of Legislative Assembly (MLA) supported the community forest concept to help resolve conflict, and the British Columbia Ministry of Forests invited Creston to apply for a license.

Seeking to augment their wood supply, the two local sawmills approached Creston Town Council with an offer to manage the licensed area for the municipality and in turn pay about $5/m^3 to the Town. However, residents did not want an industrial forest with a façade of community control, especially after decades of conflict and public involvement. Primary water users expressed concern because Arrow Creek would be in the assigned operating area. The Creston residents' lobby group approached several other community groups with the idea of submitting a parallel proposal. Thus, two proposals were submitted for the government advertised Forest License: one from the Town and two sawmills, and one from the group of other local stakeholders. The Town quickly changed sides to join the residents' proposal group. The residents' lobby group considered partnering with the mills as well; however, it was decided that this presented a conflict of interest.

On June 1, 1997 a provincial announcement was made offering the community group a Forest License. The CVFC was also established in June following some debate among the members of the residents' lobby group about organizational structure. The group decided that a regis-tered society model was inappropriate because of concerns that it would be too easy to change the mandate. A corporation with share-holders would have better control over the directorship and, therefore, management of the company. The original board of directors was assembled with five shareholders: Town of Creston; the Regional Dis-trict of Central Kootenay; the Lower Kootenay Indian Band; the East Kootenay Environmental Society; and the Creston Area Economic Devel-opment Society. Each shareholder had a director on the board, and five more at-large directors were selected from the community. The corpor-ation's constitution prohibited shareholder dividends. Profits would instead be reinvested into community projects. The first board was decidedly "green" owing to strong suspicion in the community and strong protectionist values. Their initial list of goals and objectives reflected this orientation (Table 5.1).

A 15-year, volume-based, non-replaceable Forest License was awarded in October 1997 (Smith 2004). The 12,800-hectare (31,600-acre)

Table 5.1 *Creston Valley Forest Corporation original goals and objectives**

1. To develop an ecosystem-based, ecologically responsible philosophy of forest stewardship that respects all forest values and functions.
2. To encourage involvement and to inform the public in the management of forest resources.
3. To provide local employment in harvesting, silviculture (reforestation), forestry and milling sectors.
4. To develop a local log market and examine the feasibility of a log sort yard.
5. To encourage education and training in all aspects of sustainable forestry.
6. To provide the maintenance of water quality, quantity and flow regime of all streams and lakes within the operating area of FL A54214.
7. To use existing local facilities for primary breakdown. Local refers to an area from Yahk to Riondel.
8. To provide a timber supply for existing value-added enterprises and to provide a timber supply as an incentive to promote local, value-added opportunities in the community.
9. To pursue "Green" (FSC) certification on all timber harvested under FL A54214.
10. To pursue incremental forestry projects as opportunities occur.
11. To pursue effective, biologically oriented methods dealing with forest health issues.

*Based on Smith (2004)

operating area included Arrow Creek and some lands adjacent to the community, and included several domestic watersheds. In all, 93% of the operating area was highly important to community water supplies. When the directors set about hiring a forest manager in March 1998, the former chairman of the PAC was hired from among the contractors who applied, owing to his experience with mediating existing local interest groups and his expertise in alternative silvicultural systems. CVFC then secured a start-up loan for $280,000 CAD from a local bank, which was later increased to $360,000 CAD in order to start logging. The directors developed the structure and policies of the corporation, while the forest manager (at that time the sole employee) planned operations. By spring of 1998, CVFC was seeking consultants to undertake hydrology and soil stability assessments as part of the required Forest Development Plan and Cutting Permit.

Creston residents were unsettled that a new forest company, albeit a community forest, would be allowed to log in Arrow Creek once again. Numerous residents wrote letters to the newspaper and local watershed protection groups were formed: the Erikson Water Users

Society, Water Action Group and the local Improvement District were all involved and were opposed to logging in the watershed. The local mills did not support the community forest either, because they had lost direct access to local wood and felt they had not been supported by the community. CVFC held public meetings before the Forest Plan was completed in September 1999. The central theme that emerged was to prohibit logging in Arrow Creek. Discussions turned to the fact that the preservation campaign had already failed and that not logging in Arrow Creek was not a practical option given CVFC's assigned operating area. The CVFC confirmed residents' concerns and challenged them to monitor CVFC operations closely. CVFC literally told residents "don't trust us" until CVFC had proved themselves and delivered on their very green goals and objectives.

The CVFC wanted to avoid Arrow Creek until they had demonstrated sound partial cutting practices and earned community trust; however, the reality of operational constraints set in immediately. Initial reconnaissance found stands of lodgepole pine that had been badly damaged during the winter of 1996–97. CVFC planned to log the damaged stands to salvage the timber, and obtained a cutting permit that included one cutblock in Arrow Creek. Partial cutting techniques were used throughout even though Ministry of Forests staff urged them to clear-cut the stand. CVFC felt that using clear-cutting – even winter-damaged top-broken pine in the contentious watershed – would diminish organizational credibility. Reconnaissance also revealed the legacy of past industrial harvesting. Much of the operating area had been heavily cutover and burned several times. Timber stocks were limited. Not surprisingly, Arrow Creek had the best standing timber because it had been protected for several decades. The CVFC focused on undertaking partial cutting outside Arrow Creek to build community trust. By 2002 several hundred hectares had been harvested using a variety of partial cutting systems. CVFC staff then toured their critics through the woods to show them the practical results of their green goals and objectives. Two more cutblocks were later harvested with the approval of directors who represented former opponents: Water Action Network, Erickson Improvement District and Erickson Water Users Society.

Nonetheless, the CVFC struggled financially. They had started a log sort yard, which soon proved too costly. At the time, excessively large industry-oriented stumpage rates, poor access to markets and low log prices further minimized potential profits. CVFC hired Silva Forest Consultants in 2002 to develop an ecosystem-based plan and maps for future management, and to address fire interface responsibilities. These tasks supported the goals and objectives promised to the community, but added costs that (at that time) were not recognized by the provincial stumpage appraisal system. In February 2003, a corporate manager was added to assist the forest manager in improving the struggling small business.

With the end date of their Forest License on the horizon (October 1, 2012), CVFC worked to convert their volume-based industrial Forest License into a long-term area-based Community Forest Agreement license with an expanded operating area. When the BC Forest Revitalization Plan was introduced in March 2003 (i.e. 20% claw back of existing industrial fiber for reallocation to small businesses and auction) CVFC began to build a relationship with Tembec – the company that would be giving up timber volume for local reallocation. CVFC expressed interest in 8,000 hectares that was contiguous to CVFC's existing operating area. CVFC's goal was to expand the annual harvest from 15,000 m^3 to 40,000 m^3, but the Ministry of Forests suggested that 25,000 m^3 was more realistic. In August 2004, the Ministry of Forests (BCMOF 2004) invited CVFC to delineate a suitable expansion area should they be awarded a Community Forest Agreement license. The expansion could not come too soon. In March 2005 the existing CVFC operating area was further reduced by the BC Ministry of Sustainable Resource Management when the Arrow Creek headwaters were designated as a protected area for endangered caribou. Though the community forest did not oppose the designation, it posed yet another restriction on CVFC operations. The CVFC was finally awarded a Probationary Community Forest Agreement in November 2008 (British Columbia Ministry of Forests and Range, BCMFR 2008). Consultations with First Nations and industry led to the expansion of the Arrow Creek operating area from 12,800 to 18,000 ha; however, the annual harvest remained at 15,000 m^3.

Despite adversity, CVFC has adapted and continues to practice ecosystem-based forestry. Public participation continues through the board of directors, open board meetings and public open houses. The corporation provides local employment; between 10 and 25 people are employed through logging, transportation, technical assistance and road construction contracted locally. The local mills retain right of first refusal on CVFC logs and 75% of CVFC logs are sold locally or regionally. Well over $1 million in stumpage fees has been paid to the province; CVFC contributes about $1.1 million directly into the local economy each year. And Arrow Creek's water quality and quantity have been maintained – a primary and original objective of those who started the community forest.

IMPLEMENTATION CHALLENGES

The development of a community forest in Creston can be viewed as evolving through several collaborative process stages (see Selin and Chavez 1995). The Creston Valley initiative began during an antecedent stage of crisis where the initial leadership and vision emerged for source water and habitat protection, and forest-based and agricultural resource development, based on local control of natural resources. The local movement for a community forest as a whole then went through a period of increasingly formal relations and processes where stakeholders were identified and problem definitions were set, before moving into direction setting and the establishment of goals and ground rules, and the eventual establishment of a legal organization, with delegation of roles and tasks. As institutions were formalized, CVFC eventually reached an operational stage to realize both benefits and challenges, and to monitor outcomes, which would inform future decisions. While it is helpful to view implementation as a series of stages, in practice such processes are non-linear and complicated by sub-stages and sub-processes, multiple iterations, feedbacks and cross-scale interactions typical of social-ecological systems (Olsson *et al.* 2004). As outlined in Chapter 2 of this book, community forestry implementation challenges and conflict must be considered with reference to the complex array of ecological, social, political and economic forces that influence unfolding collaborations. That is, there is a need to explicitly ground collaborative processes in a context, in keeping with an integrated approach (Mitchell 2002). Below, we present some critical challenges to implementing community forestry in Creston.

Weak support

Local support for community forestry in Creston was low from the outset. The community had a long history of public involvement in forest management through the PAC and later CORE participation processes, but there was not widespread community support. The idea for a community forest was not presented to the community until a small group of people had worked out some of the details and formed partnerships. Primary water users were staunchly opposed to any form of logging in Arrow Creek, and the strong preservation movement for caribou habitat and a rare strain of cutthroat trout overshadowed economic wishes, even with the local mill closure and job loss. Across the province, greater awareness of the community forest concept was low as there were only a few municipal forests during the early 1990s (i.e. in Mission, British Columbia), and provincial community forest programs had not yet begun.

The short duration of the proposal development stage for the community forest, and limited resident participation, had a direct negative influence on the level of community awareness and support. Having lobbied for decades, the community had strong government contacts, which quickly propelled the initiative to an advanced planning stage. The downside was that there was little time to build common local understanding for community forestry. A small number of residents were involved with shareholder selection and application preparation. Although the planning group achieved some community involvement through having community stakeholders, there were no early opportunities for wider public participation in the form of town hall meetings, workshops or surveys. While well-intentioned, a select few individuals framed the issues and set the direction for the community forest, which raises questions of representation and no doubt contributed to the lack of trust among residents. This process contrasted with former PAC and CORE processes, which afforded substantial local input over longer time periods. Though elected and appointed municipal and regional government representatives were involved, the project advanced without broad community buy-in.

Maintaining First Nations support was a key challenge. While CVFC representatives were optimistic that bridges could be built, relations between CVFC and First Nations were admittedly strained owing to a past personal conflict. When research interviews were conducted in 2005, Lower Kootenay Indian Band were not attending CVFC board meetings, but the First Nation had not formally withdrawn as a shareholder either. The Lower Kootenay Indian Band was still actively reviewing all CVFC planning and management documents and providing feedback. However, band governance, land claim negotiations, and the 20% provincial forest redistribution represented parallel processes that created competing priorities and divergent interests to further limit First Nation participation. Those interviewed from the CVFC and Ministry of Forests agreed that a stronger rapport with the Lower Kootenay Indian Band was paramount to obtaining a Community Forest Agreement and expanded operating area. By 2008 the Lower Kootenay Indian Band had formally withdrawn as a stakeholder in the CVFC.

Local competition for tenure

The two local mills were interested in the Forest License offered to the community as a way to increase access to resources amidst the regional shortage of timber supply. The mills provided local employment and presented Town Council with a management proposal that would minimize municipal obligations (and therefore control). This was troubling for residents who did not want industry control of Arrow Creek. The planning committee's quick organization and application offended mill managers who perceived community competition as infringing on their long-held, although informal, sphere of influence. Thus, BCMOF had to consider more than one application from the "community," both of which would create local benefits and, potentially, further conflict. This triangle of relations among forest management stakeholders created animosity between community leaders, whether in community development activities or in local enterprise, all of whom were local residents alleging to have the best interest of the "community" in mind. Mixed community identity and power relations point to the challenge for senior government in finding proposals that best represent and respect local power relations while providing maximum benefit from public resources.

Contentious area and degraded site conditions

Interview participants explained that the CVFC's operable land base included a number of contentious watersheds, viewscapes and wildlife habitats that were important to residents. Some areas were described as "thoroughly trashed" from previous logging. Ecosystem-based forest management was expensive, but was more acceptable to residents. The sensitive nature of the operating area, degraded site conditions and difficult site characteristics (e.g. steep slopes) challenged efforts to devise a feasible forest management plan that would not compromise ecosystem-based principles.

In the process, continuing to build community trust and support was commonly cited as the biggest challenge when tenure was awarded. The prospect of a new "corporation" logging in Arrow Creek made residents uneasy. As one participant noted, residents, environmental watchdog groups and local water users initially rejected the community forest:

> It was a very contentious thing to be doing, to be logging in a watershed which represents so much of the wealth of Creston. *CVFC representative*

The CVFC eventually held meetings to gauge public concerns and take suggestions. Among the concerns, local people expressed concern over water siltation, giardia, and impacts on fish and wildlife habitat associated with logging, as well as the potential for increased all-terrain vehicle traffic. Residents remained skeptical and the forest development plan took almost 2 years to complete – a delay which did little to help build support.

Weak provincial support and bureaucracy

Some very early champions of the CVFC felt that the community forest was not genuinely supported by the local Ministry of Forests and provincial government. There was perceived variation in the level of commitment shown by government representatives. Some related this to the culture of the local Ministry of Forests district office and overriding industry–government associations. CVFC representatives stated that they received little technical support from the Ministry of Forests in preparing the first cutting permit, which contributed to unusually high stumpage rates and subsequent debt. Inexperience and idealistic ecosystem-based goals were admittedly partly to blame, but the feeling remained that in the early days of the community forest the Ministry of Forests did not show the courtesy of advising CVFC of their mistakes prior to issuing the cutting permit. Representatives from the local Ministry of Forests office stated that community forests did not receive special attention and are "handled as any other licensee." Despite the well-intentioned style of agency officials who were likely trying not to play favorites, it shows how new ideas are sometimes difficult to accommodate under existing management arrangements. Ministry staff also stated that technical assistance and consultation was a challenge for provincial officials given the amount of time and "hand-holding" required. To be fair, dealing with community tenures presented different challenges for Ministry of Forests officials, who were used to handling industrial tenures and a small number of familiar companies. Policy innovation requires that officials at all levels expand their mental models of routines and operations from "this is how we do things around here" to "this is how we *could* do things."

Unrealistic goals and objectives

Participants described some of CVFC's initial goals and objectives as "lofty," "very green" and "idealistic." While CVFC delivered on many of the goals and objectives, they realized the implications of being a novice organization. The costs of following an ecosystem-based forestry plan were prohibitive as this was not (at the time) supported by existing provincial stumpage policy. It was learned that a log sort yard was not feasible with a provincially assigned annual allowable cut of only 15,000 m^3. Local markets for certain species of wood were non-existent, and some mills initially would not buy CVFC logs out of protest. One participant acknowledged: "We should have learned how to crawl, before we learned how to walk, before we tried running. We went right into running and fell on our face."

Inadequate financing and skills

The corporation was set up before tenure was actually awarded, and CVFC began with no money from its shareholders. The organizing process advanced so rapidly that financing was postponed until tenure had been awarded. Early lack of funding escalated into more serious problems at later stages as CVFC accrued significant debt before generating any revenue. Financial challenges and poor management were cited as being directly related to inexperience. CVFC had personnel with ample experience in using different silvicultural systems to implement difficult and complex landscape level management; however, people with business experience were also needed to balance forest management expertise. The small operating budget limited staffing. The corporation started out in a debt position and continued under growing debt due to high stumpage fees and an unprofitable log sort yard. Many participants felt there was a steep learning curve and that significant organizational learning had to occur for the corporation to become efficient and profitable. CVFC staff and directors had to learn about log marketing, the US timber scaling system and Canadian manufacturing requirements for timber in order to access export markets for locally undesirable logs.

The CVFC worked to demonstrate that their forestry practices would protect non-timber values as a primary concern, but residents remained critical of logging in Arrow Creek. Poor business management had its costs. Some residents were critical that CVFC was becoming a liability to the community. CVFC staff felt there continued to be a lack of awareness in the community of the wider benefits of ecologically sensitive forestry. Interview participants from all sides agreed that the inability to present substantial and tangible economic benefits to the community undermined support, leaving residents to focus only on the challenges. The Ministry of Forests confirmed also that local industry had "complained" about CVFC's conservative harvesting, and that the harvestable timber supply was not being fully utilized.

Unsupportive stumpage appraisal system

During the first round of interviews in June 2005, the unsupportive stumpage appraisal system was identified as the toughest challenge. Designed for industry by industry, the system rewarded forestry practices contrary to ecosystem-based management. For example, road building and regeneration silviculture could be written down against stumpage fees; CVFC's first cutting permit purposefully minimized road building and maximized partial cutting, which negated road and regeneration costs. CVFC paid $39.75/m^3 for the first harvest; at the time industrial licenses could pay as low as 25 cents/m^3 in British Columbia (R. Greschner, personal communication, February 2006). The stumpage system also weighed heavily against CVFC logging methods because it did not adequately recognize the higher costs associated with intensively managing for wider forest values, which was needed to work in sensitive and controversial areas of Arrow Creek and Town of Creston viewscapes. Community forest practices that supported fire interface, water quality, fish and wildlife habitat, and aesthetics were not sufficiently compensated under the industrial system. CVFC staff had to learn how to "manipulate" the stumpage appraisal system to "make it work" for small-scale, ecoforestry practices: "If you don't play the game the same as the majors do, you're going to get beat up badly." CVFC hired an industry consultant to help them reduce stumpage rates.

When CVFC initially presented their stumpage problems to the provincial government, a provincial official fully agreed that the policy needed to be changed but replied: "You're not the one the [Forest] Minister has lunch with." As a local organization, CVFC staff and board members felt they had little chance of influencing government and forest industry elites – that community forestry was excluded from the provincial forest policy network. CVFC participants stated that they often met resistance from the "old guard" of industry, government and pro-industry residents. The perceived resistance was attributed to the novelty of community forests in British Columbia, environmental stereotypes of community forestry and its supporters, the biases of traditional scientific forestry training, and collusion. Working through the then newly established BC Community Forest Association, CVFC was advocating strongly for change to mismatched stumpage policies based on their unfortunate experiences – to change the rules of "the game."

Poor markets and no economy of scale

Competing in British Columbia's forest sector was challenging for a small business. Low log prices and accessing log markets were notable challenges. CVFC gives right of first refusal on logs to the local mills and prefers to sell locally; however, the mills would not initially buy from them, and when CVFC started the mills could only use certain species (this relationship and product mix evolved over time, however, so that the local mills have been the steadiest customers). Regional and international markets could absorb CVFC logs but transportation costs were high. CVFC tried to establish a local market for their logs but soon realized that they did not have the economy of scale to run a log sort yard. It was often difficult to wait for markets to improve as the CVFC needed steady revenues to maintain daily operations. Practical management constraints sometimes required cutting when markets were poor or when stumpage rates were high, such as cutting before pests invaded, or cutting due to minimum Annual Allowable Cut requirements (the latter constraint has since been lifted). Conversely, vertically integrated mills could take a loss on log sales and compensate with manufacturing revenues. For the community forest, lack of diversity in revenues contributed to low economic stability and debt accumulation.

Biophysical context: difficult operating area and site conditions

The CVFC's small operating area placed logistical constraints on forest management. As one CVFC representative noted:

> When we got our operating area, I could see that [it included] areas that nobody else wanted 'cause they were either thoroughly trashed, or else they were so controversial that nobody [in the forest industry] wanted them.

The CVFC's initial ecosystem-based plan estimated the "potential timber management land base" at 4,043 hectares; 2,331 hectares of this was classified as "undeveloped" (Leslie *et al.* 2003: 57). Protected areas, caribou reserve, culturally sensitive areas and generally poor site conditions due to previous logging and fire significantly reduced CVFC's operable land base and, therefore, timber supply. CVFC did not want to log in sensitive areas or use different practices that might compromise ecosystem-based principles. Consensus among participants was that CVFC needed an expanded operating area and increased AAC. Moreover, the provincial AAC redistribution and land claims had the Lower

Kootenay Indian Band in competition with CVFC for forest lands near Creston, which represented a conflict for both sides. The Lower Kootenay Indian Band expressed concerns with areas that CVFC and Tembec had discussed for reallocation to CVFC. This created uncertainty for the future of the CVFC and the possible expansion of the operating area.

Poor timber profiles and forest health did not offer a good supply of merchantable timber either. Much of the remaining timber was of low quality, a poor variety or immature. Some of the most valuable stands were located in contentious areas and so were not eligible for harvest by CVFC standards. Snow- and beetle-damaged wood was salvaged to improve forest health irrespective of current markets for particular species (a potential liability). CVFC participants said that their concerns for the operating area and new tenure were slow to be heard. It was difficult to get the attention of provincial representatives who had the authority to influence policy for positive change.

It is important to point out that despite an overall frustration with process issues prior to 2004, CVFC and the local District office of Ministry of Forests and Range currently share an excellent rapport. Follow-up correspondence with both parties confirmed that CVFC is pleased with the current level of support they receive from Ministry staff and management. The provincial agency is also contributing to the ongoing success of two neighboring community forests. Such progress is a testament to the persistence and hard work of both sides.

CONCLUSION

The CVFC case study shows that several multi-scaled factors were influential at different stages, and that challenges mutually evolved as implementation advanced. For example, lack of support for community forestry was a pervasive and persistent political challenge among local residents, local industry, government and even CVFC shareholders. This led to challenges in other domains and later stages in the process: poor access to potential local log markets due to unsupportive industry; financial debt due to lack of technical understanding and assistance; and personality conflicts within CVFC leading to damaged rapport and loss of trust between stakeholders, to name a few.

Following the decision to act, local people and groups with different values yet similar interests coalesced around a shared environmental/resource problem. Partnerships and institutions developed as the community organized. Collaborative information generation and strategic planning was undertaken in preparation for securing tenure and increased local control over forests resources. Government and stake-holder negotiation resulted in the formation of a functional organiza-tion that could assume management responsibilities. The CVFC advanced to operations and continues to implement programs and policies that reflect organizational and community (and provincial for that matter) goals and objectives. While experiencing increased stabil-ity and efficiency, CVFC is still embracing and adapting to new manage-ment responsibilities as they arise. For example, the formal withdrawal of the Lower Kootenay Indian Band presents a critical challenge for CVFC given the ethical and operational importance of maintaining positive relations with First Nations neighbors. Remaining CVFC share-holders continue to work closely with the Ministry of Forests towards ensuring a future for community forestry in Creston.

Notably, early challenges were mainly of a strategic nature and involved information gathering, developing understanding, navigating political environments and the initial development of the organization. Operationalizing the community forest introduced new and different challenges, many of which were economic and related to day-to-day operations and management of what is essentially a small business. Learning and adaptation throughout the process were thus key organ-izational responses to change and uncertainty. This enabled CVFC to overcome many challenges and achieve success in instances where both ambition and caution could have led to outright failure of the initiative.

REFERENCES

British Columbia Ministry of Forests (BCMOF) (2004). News release: Kootenays benefit from community forest opportunity. August 11, 2004. BCMOF. Avail-able at http://www2.news.gov.bc.ca/archive/2001-2005/2004FOR0037-000642.htm. Accessed April 4, 2011.
British Columbia Ministry of Forests and Range (BCMFR) (2008). News release: Creston to benefit from community forest. Available at http://www2.news.gov.bc.ca/news_releases_2005-2009/2008FOR0145-001668.htm. Accessed April 4, 2011.
Leslie, E., Bradley, T. and Hammond, H. (2003). *Creston Valley Forest Corporation Initial Ecosystem-Based Plan*. Silva Forest Foundation.
Mitchell, B. (2002). *Resource and Environmental Management*. Harlow, UK and New York: Prentice Hall/Pearson Education.
Olsson, P., Folke, C. and Hahn, T. (2004). Social-ecological transformation for ecosystem management: The development of adaptive co-management of a wetland landscape in southern Sweden. *Ecology and Society* **9**(4): 2.
Selin, S. and Chavez, D. (1995). Developing a collaborative model for environmental-planning and management. *Environmental Management* **19**(2): 189–95.
Smith, J. (2004). Community trust and watershed management in Creston, British Columbia, Canada. In Baumgartner, D. (ed.) *Human Dimensions of Family, Farm,*

and Community Forestry International Symposium. Pullman, WA: Washington State University, pp. 155–58.

Statistics Canada (2006). Community profiles. Available at http://www.statcan.gc.ca. Accessed July 1, 2011.

Sunderman, R. (2003). Establishment of the Creston log sort yard: Case study. BC Journal of Ecosystems and Management. 3(1): 1–6.

Town of Creston (2001). Town of Creston homepage. Available at http://www.Crestonbc.com. Accessed: January 2, 2012.

Town of Creston (2004). Town of Creston homepage. Available at http://www.Crestonbc.com. Accessed: July 1, 2011.

Town of Creston (2005). *Official Community Plan: Consolidated Bylaw 1532.* Creston, BC: Town of Creston.

6

Contested forests and transition in two Gulf Island communities

In this chapter we provide a comparative illustration of barriers to implementing community forests on British Columbia's Pacific coast. We recount the parallel experiences of two small Gulf Island communities that have been unsuccessful thus far in establishing community forests after four decades of struggle with off-island (and indeed on-island) forest interests. The communities on Denman Island and Cortes Island appear similar with respect to certain internal characteristics and events; they share a similar settlement history unfolding from the earliest First Nations peoples to non-Aboriginal homesteaders, to back-to-the-landers and, most recently, amenity migrants. This succession is linked to transitioning rural resource economies and evolving demographic profiles and, in particular, the emergence of a formally educated and "graying" middle class. Each island is politically unorganized and has endured social conflict related to industrial forest development and local efforts to get involved in forest governance. Both community forest initiatives emerged from informal grassroots monitoring committees during the 1980s and adopted the principles of ecosystem-based management early on (hiring the same consultant in fact). Just as in the case of Creston (see Chapter 5), the roots of each initiative and the notion of increasing local control long pre-date formal provincial efforts during the late 1990s to create the BC Community Forest Agreement program.

Each community has yet to fully establish a community forest, but for different reasons. Key differences lie in the challenges each experienced with community mobilization, local institutions, stakeholder involvement, and the decision-making structures and processes used to govern forest ecosystems. Although each failed to secure full control of the contested forest lands, to say this was *the* main stumbling block would be a gross oversimplification. The nuances of local collective processes and structures for community-based management are more visible through micro- and comparative analyses (Gibson *et al.* 2000). Key events and factors constraining implementation in rural settings of transition and contestation will be presented for each case, leading into a synthesis and discussion of some critical challenges pertaining to institutional issues in First Nations relations, local politics and the latent growth control agenda in the community forest movement.

CASE 1: DENMAN ISLAND

Denman Island is located in the Strait of Georgia between Vancouver Island and the western coast of British Columbia. With a land area of 81 km^2, the island is almost entirely privately owned (93%), save for the Crown lands at Boyle Point and Filongly Park (Table 6.1). Historically, Salish indigenous people from nearby Comox made summer camps on Denman, but few First Nations people reside on the island now and there are no reserve lands.

Located within the Regional District[1] of Comox-Strathcona, Denman Island does not have municipal status but is organized under the Island's Trust Council, which administers community planning needs (zoning and by-laws, services, environmental protection) for 13 associated trust area islands and one island municipality. Under the Province of British Columbia's 1989 *Islands Trust Act*:

> The object of the Trust is to preserve and protect the Trust Area and its unique amenities and environment for the benefit of the residents of the Trust Area and of British Columbia generally, in cooperation with municipalities, regional districts, improvement districts, other persons and organizations and the government of British Columbia. (Islands Trust Council 2011)

Each island has a three-person local trust committee responsible for working with their communities to develop policy and regulations.

Denman Island has 2,170 residents (+9.4% from 2001 to 2006) (Statistics Canada 2006), although the permanent year-round population is estimated at 1,250. Like other Gulf Islands, Denman is a summer haven for urban dwellers and tourists. In recent years there has been an influx of retirees. Notably, about half of the population is above age 55 (Statistics Canada 2006). Agriculture, forestry and fishing were traditionally important following European settlement in the 1870s. However, the rising significance of other industries coincides with the

Table 6.1 *Geographical and organizational attributes, Denman Island and Cortes Island*

	Denman Island	Cortes Island
Island size	81 km^2	136 km^2
CF origins	Early 1980s	Early 1980s
Proposed CF land	~1,700 ha	~6,500 ha
Property	Private: 93% (33% by forest industry)	Private: 48% (34% small holdings; 14% industry)
	Provincial: 7%	Provincial Crown: 39%
		Government protected areas: 10%
		First Nations: 3%
Administrative structure	Cooperative	Partnership
Main industries	Tourism, agriculture, services	Tourism, aquaculture, services

island's changing character. The majority of Denman's residents now work in health and education, government, business and management, services and manufacturing (Statistics Canada 2001). There is also a diverse community of artists and artisans at the core of Denman's vibrant tourism industry. About 10% of the total working population (about 109 out of 1,090 people) works in agriculture and resource industries, and more than half of these (65 individuals) are farmers. Less than 4.5% of Denman's working population was employed by a resource industry, indicating that still fewer workers were in forestry (Statistics Canada 2006). Denman Island is not a "blue-collared" rural resource community that depends on forestry.

EMERGENCE OF THE DENMAN COMMUNITY FOREST COOPERATIVE

The movement for local control of Denman Island forests was ignited by a major private land sale in May 1995. Long-term landowners Weldwood of Canada Ltd. sold a 1,700-hectare (4,200-acre) tract of forest land – nearly one-third of the island – to John Hancock Timber Resources Group of Boston, USA. With no municipal government on the island, for many years the harvesting activities of Weldwood had been monitored by the Denman Forestry Committee (DFC), a sub-committee of the Denman Island Resident's and Ratepayer's Association (DIRRA). There was sporadic logging on Weldwood's land, and residents freely used the property as common green space. Meetings with the new owners revealed plans to clear-cut the property commencing in November 1995, which generated great concern among residents. As an immediate response, members of the Denman Forestry Committee branched off to develop a buy-out plan.

A public meeting was held and initial community consensus was for forest conservation, but there were many different ideas about how this should happen. By December 1995, public meetings had produced three paths of action to be pursued by separate groups: (1) continue monitoring Hancock's harvesting processes; (2) buy the land from Hancock; and (3) co-manage the lands with Hancock in order to influence practices. All three separate initiatives advanced in parallel.

Hancock indicated a willingness to work with the community to address local desires for sustainable forestry and a possible land sale. The "Buy-out Group" was the most productive local group. They sought funding and gathered information, and brought in practitioners and academics as guest speakers at local meetings. Based on the ecosystem-based planning principles of Silva Forestry Consultants, the Buy-out Group became the Denman Forestry Initiative (DFI) in May of 1996 exactly one year after the land sale to Hancock.

The first of many heated protests also came in May 1996 when concerned residents interrupted clear-cut logging operations on Hancock's lands (DCFC 2001). Residents, who were alarmed at the apparent rate of harvesting, attempted to stall the process as Denman Forestry Initiative was still in exploration and data-collection mode. Despite the interruption, Hancock reaffirmed its support for Denman Forestry Initiative's purchasing plans in August 1996 (DCFC 2001). However, an inflammatory letter was sent by the Denman Forestry Committee to Hancock's CEO, angering executives who threatened to deal exclusively with Denman Forestry Initiative.

Having secured grant monies from a provincial fund intended for forest renewal (i.e. Forest Renewal BC), the Denman Forestry Initiative commissioned Silva Forestry Consultants to conduct the long-awaited ecosystem-based landscape planning and landscape assessments of Hancock's lands. In May 1997, Denman Forestry Initiative held a public meeting to discuss the appropriateness of a cooperative management structure to own and manage a community forest on Denman Island (DCFC 2001). Residents were open to the idea of a cooperative venture because of the history of volunteer cooperative efforts that went into organizing on-island community work. Every indication was that Hancock was prepared to sell to the Denman Forestry Initiative. Then on June 30, 1997, two years after purchase, Hancock suddenly announced the sale of their forest lands to a numbered company called 4064 Ltd. Members of the community were shocked to say the least.

The sudden change of ownership set off a rapid course of events with many negative outcomes for community management goals. The new owner began moving logging equipment across to the island the day after the sale, and protesting Denman residents turned away work crews. Two hundred Denman residents then attended an emergency meeting to discuss the land sale. Video was shown of the new owner's clear-cut logging practices on Gabriola Island, another Gulf Island. This generated serious concern among residents. Unanimous support was given for continued efforts to buy and manage the land. Some residents formed the Community Action Network (CAN) to engage 4064 Ltd. logging crews in non-violent protests, which happened daily and would happen for several months.

Given the level of conflict, Denman representatives managed to meet with the Premier of British Columbia, officials from the Ministry of Forests, and Forest Renewal BC on July 8, 1997 to seek backing for their buy-out plan (DCFC 2001). The Premier supported the idea but pressed the community to develop a credible business plan, which was already a work in progress. The tentative business plan addressed a cross-section of community interests, including timber harvesting, residential land development, ecoforestry education, fundraising for conservation and an investment program for community ownership of forest resources. The day after the meeting with the Premier, 4064 Ltd. began road building on some sensitive hilly terrain without necessary development permits from the Islands Trust. Angry Denman residents contacted 4064 Ltd. and informed the Islands Trust of the violation. Yet 4064 Ltd. continued to work under legal advice that industrial logging rules superseded the Islands Trust by-laws. Lawyers from all sides became involved while the road construction continued.[2]

After some heated disputes between loggers and residents, Denman Forestry Initiative representatives finally met with 4064 Ltd. on July 23, 1997 (DCFC 2001). Denman Forestry Initiative representatives made clear their intentions to purchase the land, but accepted no responsibility for the protests of the Community Action Network. 4064 Ltd. then shared its own Denman Island forest data with Denman Forestry Initiative representatives, and for the first time it was apparent that detailed forest inventory information *did* actually exist – Hancock had never provided such data to the community. 4064 Ltd. appeared to be cooperating, agreeing to Denman Forestry Committee monitoring and agreeing to hold off on logging until August 4, 1997 to enable

Denman Forestry Initiative to prepare a purchase offer. However, 4064 Ltd. also clearly indicated their interest in the timber, having already made arrangements for its sale.

It took one month for Denman Forestry Initiative to secure a loan in order to make a formal offer to 4064 Ltd. During that time community meetings continued for the establishment of a local cooperative organization, which had been put on hold in the scramble that ensued with the change of land ownership. The blockades also continued. Some Denman residents had also gone to the British Columbia Legislature to stage a protest for forest protection. At the same time, the Islands Trust was hurrying the enactment of sustainable forestry by-laws aimed at regulating 4064's logging. Denman Forestry Initiative made a cash offer of $16.5 million CAD to 4064 Ltd. in late August, 1997, which 4064 Ltd. rejected because it was seen as too low, and because the company had partners in log trading and sawmilling who very much wanted the wood (Beattie 1997). Discouraged, the community held a meeting to realign divergent community actions and discuss plans to form a cooperative.

In short order, the Denman Community Forest Cooperative (DCFC) was finally officially formed on November 25, 1997 (DCFC 2001). Months later in May 1998 the cooperative received the Ecosystem-Based Landscape Analysis and Plan from Silva Forestry Consultants. Acknowledging missed opportunity and local disappointment, in the final paragraphs of the assessment the consultants recommended that the Denman community

> should [still] endeavour to obtain ownership of the 4064 Lands as soon as possible, regardless of the condition of the forest on those lands at this time. Forty years will pass very quickly. It would be a gift to future generations of islanders to pass on the foundation for ecologically responsible community forestry, rather than the pain of divisive and painful conflict. (Bradley *et al.* 1998: 54–55)

Nearly 3 years after Hancock's purchase, the community held a strategic meeting in June 1998 to establish long-term goals, prioritize activities and determine a clear vision for the DCFC. However, as 4064's logging was well under way, the forest lands of most interest had been considerably reduced. Another purchase offer was made in July 1998 based on diminishing forest resources. On August 5, 1998, the Denman Community Forest Cooperative decided to break off talks with 4064 Ltd. owing to the apparent futility of the process (DCFC 2001).

In the months that followed, hopes for a community forest on Denman Island dissolved. The rate of harvesting and volume of timber that had been removed negated any reasonable immediate purchase of the land for a community forest. Relations descended further into conflict; local efforts focused on disrupting logging activities, and protests became especially heated. By-laws on sustainable forest land use finally came into effect in May of 1999 (DCFC 2001). But the cumulative effect of these actions was that several legal battles were being fought simultaneously between 4064 Ltd., the Islands Trust and individual residents, while logging continued.

By June 2005, 4064's Denman Island properties were in the process of being sold to various new owners (i.e. North Denman Lands Inc.). Residents were considering a controversial development proposal for a major part of the formerly proposed community forest lands. This would add several new homes in the most scenic areas, with a small portion of land earmarked for a community forest or public green space. Six years on, local efforts have helped to create a public–private partnership to conserve 750 hectares of the formerly disputed private lands and adjacent Crown land parcels, which will ultimately augment the BC provincial parks and protected areas system (British Columbia Ministry of Environment, BCMOE 2010). Given this (albeit positive) outcome, the prospect of having a working community forest is now a distant possibility (Figure 6.1).

CASE 2: KLAHOOSE FIRST NATION AND CORTES ECOFORESTRY SOCIETY PARTNERSHIP, CORTES ISLAND

Located at the entrance to Desolation Sound in the Strait of Georgia, Cortes Island is the northernmost Gulf Island. The Island is about 136 km^2 and has an irregular shoreline (Silva Forest Foundation 1996). Cortes Island has a variable terrain that ranges from steep-sloped insular uplands in the north, to relatively low-lying flat lands in the south (Cortes Ecoforestry Society, CES 2002). Much of the central island is characterized by a mix of rocky hills and well-drained basins of productive forest land.

Homesteaders first began to settle on Cortes Island during the late 1800s and early 1900s. Subsequently, much of the island was clearcut and burned as the old growth forests were cleared for agriculture (CES 2002). Given the steep and isolating topography in the north, settlement concentrated in the southern parts of the island. These lands represented the best sites for homesteading from the standpoint of

Figure 6.1 A simple handmade sign at the end of a driveway along the main road on Denman Island reads: "A Supporter – Denman Island Community Forest" (photo: R. Bullock).

slope and productivity, and not surprisingly, forest growth. The timber company MacMillan Bloedel began to purchase these prime lands from homesteading families in the 1950s and 1960s (Klahoose *et al.* 2000). As a result, corporate interests came to own a good portion of the most productive lands on the island.

Approximately 50% of the island is Crown land (39% or 5,305 ha) and government protected areas (10% or 1,428 ha) (Silva Forest Foundation 1996). Another 34% (4,714 ha) rests in a number of small private holdings. Major forest interests have long owned about 14% (1,876 ha) of Cortes, although this has decreased slightly over time with land sales. The remaining 3% forms two Indian reserves for the Klahoose First Nation (Coast Salish) who have outstanding territorial land claims on Cortes.

Cortes Island's zoning and planning is handled by the Regional District of Comox-Strathcona. When regional governments were introduced in British Columbia during the late 1960s, the Cortes community lobbied to have the island become an electoral district unto itself, with one representative on the regional government board. Owing to its distinct representation, Cortes Island has more autonomy than many other small unorganized communities (such as Denman Island).[3]

Figure 6.2 Portable sawmill, Cortes Island (photo: R. Bullock).

While logging has been important to local history, the island's culture and economy has changed over time. The inflow of newcomers and residential development now concerns community members who want to sustain forest lands and maintain the current local culture. For example, from 2001 to 2006 the island's population increased 11.1% to 1,042 (Statistics Canada 2006). The population also swells considerably during summer months with seasonal residents and tourists who come to enjoy the enchanting island setting.

Recent socio-demographic profiles reveal a highly educated adult citizenry on Cortes who are employed mainly in professional and service industries (Statistics Canada 2001). About half of the total population is between the ages of 35 and 64, and more than 40% of them have a university education. Moreover, 44% of the working population works in health, education or business services, while agriculture, resource industries, construction and manufacturing together account for 23% of employment. Forestry is not the main economic base of the island, though many would like to see more on-island value-added opportunities developed (see Figure 6.2). There is, however, a diverse group (about 55 persons) of craftspeople, artisans, builders and laborers with links to local forestry and forest value-added (CES, personal communication, February 2006).

ORIGINS OF THE KLAHOOSE FIRST NATION/CORTES
ECOFORESTY SOCIETY PARTNERSHIP

The Cortes Island Forestry Committee (CIFC) was formed in 1988 in response to clear-cut logging on private lands by Raven Lumber and MacMillan Bloedel during the 1980s. The return of large-scale industrial logging practices contrasted greatly with what residents were used to: smaller operators, lower technology activities and slower harvest rates that appeared to have less impact on the land. Cortes Island Forestry Committee negotiated with the forest companies and Ministry of Forests to encourage ecologically responsible forestry practices. They also engaged Cortes residents to build awareness and support for community forestry through newsletters, conferences and public meetings.

Community concerns peaked in 1990 when non-Aboriginal residents joined a Klahoose-led protest of MacMillan Bloedel's plan to continue clear-cutting on lands adjacent to the Klahoose village at Squirrel Cove. It was a 2-day blockade of 125 men, women and children. Recognizing the commitment of the Cortes community, and wanting to defend their public corporate image, MacMillan Bloedel agreed to stop logging on the island until a forest plan could be developed that would satisfy community interests.

At the same time, Cortes Island Forestry Committee conducted a survey that found that 86% (n = 300) of the non-Aboriginal community wanted to maintain forest integrity as a primary value (Cortes Ecoforestry Society, CES, undated). Much at the instigation of the Klahoose Chief and Council, a good rapport between Klahoose and Cortes Island Forestry Committee was also being developed. While MacMillan Bloedel was evolving a new harvesting plan for Cortes, the Cortes Island Forestry Committee commissioned Silva Forestry Consultants in 1992 to create the Cortes Island Forest Plan. The idea actually came from the Klahoose, who had previously engaged Silva Forestry Consultants for planning work in their traditional territory. In preparing the plan and becoming familiar with ecosystem-based forestry principles, there was much internal community debate as to the true level of harvesting that would support long-term forest sustainability. MacMillan Bloedel returned in 1993 with a partial-cutting plan that was grudgingly accepted by Cortes Island Forestry Committee, and logging resumed for 5 years until 1998 (Klahoose *et al.* 2000).

However, the residents became increasingly uncomfortable with MacMillan Bloedel's operations, and the concept of community forestry was gaining momentum on a provincial scale. Numerous communities across the province were mobilizing and becoming engaged in similar community forestry negotiations and planning exercises (such as Denman Island as discussed in this chapter, and Creston as discussed in Chapter 5). Cortes residents were alarmed by two pivotal events during the winter of 1998–99: (1) without prior notice, MacMillan Bloedel sold two land parcels to "a known timber liquidator" (4064 Ltd., the company that also logged on Denman Island) and (2) the Minister of Forests allocated the Crown lands on Cortes Island to Canadian Forest Products without the legally required consultation of Klahoose or community involvement (Klahoose *et al.* 2000). These events combined to solidify desires for local control of the island's forest resources. Subsequently, the Cortes Ecoforestry Society (CES) was formed to replace the ad hoc Cortes Island Forestry Committee so that non-Aboriginal residents would be represented by an official entity.

Klahoose was actively pursuing a purchase proposal for MacMillan Bloedel parcels near Squirrel Cove when Cortes Ecoforestry Society followed their example and made their own purchase proposal to MacMillan Bloedel in November 1998. These actions gained the attention of MacMillan Bloedel's environmental vice-president, who was responsible for negotiations in heated and international renowned environmental conflict settings such as Clayoquot Sound and the Great Bear Rainforest. In March 1999, MacMillan Bloedel agreed to discontinue logging on Cortes Island until Cortes Ecoforestry Society, Klahoose and the company could resolve negotiations. Klahoose and Cortes Ecoforestry Society realized the potential difficulty of raising 15 million dollars CAD to buy MacMillan Bloedel's land and so approached the provincial government for ideas on how the land could be transferred to Cortes Island residents. Weyerhaeuser then purchased MacMillan Bloedel in fall 1999, but was bound by provincial conditions to maintain good faith negotiations with Klahoose and Cortes Ecoforestry Society (Cortes Ecoforestry Society, undated). Local purchase plans soon failed as the parties could not agree on a price, but negotiations continued.

At the same time, Klahoose and Cortes Ecoforestry Society learned of British Columbia's new 1998 Community Forest Pilot Project. The evolution of a working arrangement between the Klahoose and non-Aboriginal residents resulted in the signing of a Memorandum of Understanding in July of 1999:

> The Memorandum committed the parties to working together to implement eco-system forestry on Cortes Island's forestland base, and

> stated CES' commitment to a just resolution of Klahoose treaty rights. The
> Klahoose First Nation and CES determined to work together to obtain a
> community forest on Cortes Island. (Cortes Ecoforestry Society, undated: 1)

Community consultation with the non-Aboriginal community was undertaken by Cortes Ecoforestry Society during 1999 and 2000 for the planning and preparation of a community forest proposal, while Klahoose and Cortes Ecoforestry Society continued to work together towards the mutual goal of forming a community forest.

Negotiations between Klahoose First Nation, Cortes Ecoforestry Society and Weyerhaeuser led to the development of a very innovative three-way proposal to settle the Cortes land-use conflict. The *Cortes Initiative* proposed to convert Weyerhaeuser's Cortes lands to Crown status in exchange for Crown lands elsewhere; a community forest could then be created on the new and existing Cortes Crown land to be managed together by Klahoose and Cortes Ecoforestry Society following ecosystem-based principles (Klahoose, *et al.* 2000). The proposal was presented to the provincial government in May 2000, but was turned down by the Minister of Forests on the basis that Weyerhaeuser wanted too much compensation for their lands and that there was unresolved traditional boundary issues between Klahoose and a neighboring First Nation. Cortes Island residents felt this was a "hollow rejection" as the boundary issue had, in fact, been resolved between the two First Nations. Moreover, the proposal had First Nations, non-Aboriginal and industry support, a partnership structure, business plan, and management plan complete with up-to-date custom maps.

Klahoose First Nation then pressed forward and repackaged the Cortes Initiative as a Treaty Interim Measure. With support from the Premier, Ministry of Forests bureaucrats at the head office in Victoria were instructed to advance the process. By March 2001, a framework agreement was finally signed by Klahoose, and the provincial and federal governments:

> This agreement provided the opportunity for the Klahoose First Nation to
> apply for a community forest pilot agreement for the Crown lands on
> Cortes as a Treaty Interim Measure, including provisions for ecosystem-
> based forestry and a management partnership with CES. (Cortes
> Ecoforestry Society, undated: 2)

After a decade of protest, planning and difficult negotiations, it appeared that a community forest would finally become a reality on Cortes Island.

However, about two weeks after the Treaty Interim Measure was signed, a provincial election was called and the agreement was dropped. Cortes Ecoforestry Society also lost Klahoose support with the parallel election of a new Chief and Council during the spring of 2001. A federal declaration to expand band voting rights to off-reserve members became a significant factor in the Klahoose election. As a greater number of Klahoose members live in the Powell River area on the adjacent mainland, off-island and off-reserve votes figured in, and greatly determined, the outcome of the election. The new Chief and Council had other priorities and did not support the existing community forest movement.

Cortes Ecoforestry Society continued to explore their community forest options. Provincial representatives seemed receptive but were unwilling to support a community forest effort without First Nations support. Weyerhaeuser's coastal operations were then bought by Brascan Corporation in early 2005 and their Cortes lands were taken over by a subsidiary, Island Timberlands. While communication and negotiations over the sale and management of their Cortes holdings continued, parcels were slowly sold to independent buyers with little notice. Cortes Ecoforestry Society remained active in monitoring forest-related activities on Cortes Island, though the organization has struggled to maintain community support.

There is renewed optimism, however, that the First Nation and non-Aboriginal community on Cortes can advance their partnership efforts to form a community forest. As of June 2011, the BC government invited the Cortes Island Community Forest Advisory Group (including both First Nation and non-Aboriginal representatives) to apply for a 25-year Community Forest Agreement licence involving all Crown forests on Cortes. Once approved, a community forest management corporation will be established to equally represent the Klahoose First Nation and non-Aboriginal residents on Cortes Island (Watershed Sentinel 2011).

TWO ISLANDS, TWO OUTCOMES

Despite similarities between local movements for local control of forests on both Denman and Cortes Island, quite different challenges emerged in each setting, namely those related to local decision-making structures and planning processes through which political actors influenced human–environment interactions and outcomes (Lemos and Agrawal 2006). A focus on institutions and on deliberative and process conflicts illustrates some common experiences at early stages of development, but also sets these islands apart in terms of their major challenges to establishing the formal institutions requisite for operational community forests.

Community mobilization

The above stories illustrate that considerable grassroots effort and time from volunteers was necessary to uphold a high level of resistance to "outside" forces while the community forest concept was starting to take hold locally and provincially. It is remarkable that each initiative evolved from ad hoc grassroots monitoring committees and embarked through long community engagement processes with the same forestry consultants. One after another, each group addressed conflicts that emerged with more powerful actors. And there was no guarantee of eventual success. For the non-Aboriginal communities on both islands, this meant mobilizing scarce and scattered resources and building trust between different groups of residents. As one Cortes representative discussed:

> If you're dealing with a rural community, you're dealing with a finite population base, and the skills and experiences of those people is key to how you make [community forestry] happen, and whether it's going to happen. *Gene, Cortes Island*

Early on, informal working groups in both places met on an ad hoc basis, assigning duties as needed, without tested or legitimate community representation. However, non-Aboriginal residents on Cortes Island had the initial benefit of having a strong First Nation partner that was much more organized and resourced and could provide leadership. This leadership helped to guide and organize what was otherwise a collection of legitimately concerned and determined residents with some "good ideas."

Neither community forest initiative was unanimously supported early on. Community forests were a novel and scarcely implemented concept at the time in British Columbia and Canada. Denman Island residents were fragmented across different issues and factions, exacerbated by a collective sense of panic induced by time pressures and imminent logging. As one deflated community leader reflected:

> I don't think there was community consensus that this was, you know, everyone's chosen course. Groups of people coalesced and took it off in more directions than you can imagine. So, was there a collective vision? I don't think we got a collective vision until it became obvious that there was nothing we could do. *Nelson, Denman Island*

Like on Denman, there was enormous support for ending industrial logging on Cortes Island. The poor public image of MacMillan Bloedel, both at home and internationally throughout the mid 1990s, likely contributed to strong opposition among residents. Cortes residents wanted to increase their involvement in forest management, but it was not initially clear that a community forest was even an option. Yet unlike Denman, Cortes seemed to have the luxury of having a little more time to organize, or at least they were more calculated in their approach and took actions to organize formally early on, and so were further along. Still, support for the community forest concept took a long time to develop in both locations. A Cortes representative pointed to this challenge:

> I think the first challenge that any community encounters is informing and educating and engaging the depth of interest for a community forest within its own membership ... and I think getting people to consider and address and discuss and debate the benefits or problems associated with local control and so on. I think that's something that's been going on in the province over the last 20 years and certainly on Cortes over the last ... very close to 20 years now. *Edward, Cortes Island*

Each island's character as a summer vacation area for urbanites, as well as the influx of retirees on both islands, raises questions about the level of shared kinship, culture and history among residents thought to contribute to a strong sense of community (Jentoft 2000). New people bring new ideas, expectations and prejudices. Both islands are fast becoming vacation and bedroom communities with dispersed private land holdings often owned by urban elite, "wireless" professionals and retirees. In each of these cases, community forestry and local control were actually part of the resistance to this transition. But given this ongoing transition and the presence of several different on-island interests groups, these islands may not have such a well-defined and collective sense of community. For example, in discussing the challenges of community mobilization, participants mentioned how the number and "kinds" of newcomers made it difficult to keep everyone informed about the ongoing struggle and history of the local cause to maintain support.

Land ownership and stakeholders

There were fundamental differences in land ownership patterns between Denman and Cortes, which was significant given that ownership arrangements determined what groups were responsible for land

and forest management decisions and, ultimately, the range of actors necessarily involved. Mixed landownership on both islands created a host of actors with interests in each community, for example:

- non-Aboriginal and First Nation settlements;
- private landowners ranging from small individual residential to large foreign-owned timber companies and their subsidiaries;
- the provincial government and various provincial agencies;
- the Regional District of Comox-Strathcona;
- the Islands Trust;
- residents' and ratepayers' associations and various local ad hoc committees; and, eventually
- the community forest cooperative and society.

In theory, Denman's community forest had a more straightforward chance at success, having to deal with only one other major landowner; there were no First Nations reserves or Crown properties of import involved. It could have been a simple land deal between two organizations. But when negotiations soured, the provincial government and the Ministry of Forests were excluded, and they later took on only a minor intermediate role in trying to resolve the heated conflict. During the interview period, Ministry of Forests staff indicated that they could not speak about the conflict on Denman Island because they had no direct involvement or position (personal communication, South Island Forest District, BCMOFR, May 2005). Without engagement by the major forestry regulating agency, the situation remained a conflict between "neighboring" private landowners. The Islands Trust sided with local residents and tried to restrict timber harvesting without the legislated authority to do so. In the absence of a supportive regulatory setting, and lacking a willing seller and agreed price, it appears there was little more that could have been done to transfer the contested private forest on Denman into a community forest.

The mosaic of landownership on Cortes Island created different challenges and opportunities. There was still much unallocated Crown land on Cortes. This meant that about 40% of the island was held under provincial discretion; however, the province had a legal obligation to consult Klahoose First Nation who had outstanding land claims in their traditional territory. This gave the Klahoose considerable influence. Like Denman, there was a large corporate timber interest involved that, in the case of Cortes, was well aware of the need to work with both First Nations and non-Aboriginal groups in what would otherwise be a "socially inoperable" forest. Thus, to enable the land transfer pursued by the Klahoose–CES partnership, there were complex tenure arrangements and land transactions to be worked out between at least four main actors: MacMillan Bloedel, Ministry of Forests, Klahoose First Nation and Cortes Ecoforestry Society. Because of the number of actors involved, there were several other related processes bearing on the outcomes of negotiations. The most important perceived challenge to obtaining Klahoose–CES control was the sudden election of unsupportive governments at both the band and provincial levels in 2001. As one Cortes resident remembered:

> The ultimate downfall was simply elections all the way around. *Alice, Cortes Island*

Cortes Island residents expressed frustration with political processes that influenced them directly but that they could not control. Neither election went in favor of the formation of a Cortes community forest. In fact the loss of Klahoose support was deemed more critical than that of the provincial government, as the Cortes Ecoforestry Society was committed to forming a community forest with First Nation participation. The new Liberal government of British Columbia was not prepared to follow through with the land transfer plans of the previous government either. In the period after the 2001 elections, the Cortes Ecoforestry Society met with senior provincial and district level representatives from the Ministry of Forests as well as the Member of Legislative Assembly for the North Island, but there was no support for CES proposals for a community forest without Klahoose involvement. The problem was summed up by a Cortes resident:

> You have to have the First Nation thinking that it's a really good thing for the land and you have to have the government behind it. Without either one of those elements it's a no-go. *Vincent, Cortes Island*

A Ministry of Forests representative stated during a research interview that the province did not support the Cortes Initiative in 2000 because it was "leery of compensating companies with Crown land for private" (*Charley, BCMOF representative*). It may be that the province was reluctant to set in motion a land exchange deal that might be seen as a quick solution to numerous other land-use conflicts between First Nations, industry and community groups across the province. And at this time the province was in the nascent or nearing the "pilot" stage of setting up the Community Forest Agreement program. The Cortes Initiative was presented to the provincial cabinet as a very innovative solution to such conflicts. The same Ministry of Forests representative also stated that the Ministry had concerns for the potential administrative challenges related to the reorganization of tenures, obligations to protect Crown lands in the public interest and local capacity for forest management – all of which were in keeping with being publicly accountable and responsible. Low government support was further tied to provincial concerns for the credibility of new and existing community organizations, relinquishing power over public lands and resources to such groups, and decreased financial returns from provincially owned, yet community managed, forest land.

Local decision-making structures and processes

As unorganized territories, both islands were administered through regional government, and Cortes arguably has more autonomy than Denman (the former having a single seat and therefore one representative voice on regional government). On the other hand, Denman Island was doubly represented by the Islands Trust as an intermediary form of local government, and by a regional government representative who was also responsible for another neighboring island and part of the adjacent mainland. Unlike the case of Creston (see Chapter 5) where both municipal and regional governments were community forest shareholders with board representation, there was no provision for representatives from either local government (Islands Trust or regional government) to sit on the board of either the Cortes Ecoforestry Society or Denman Community Forest Cooperative. At the time, gaining on-island control was the principal objective of both initiatives.

Setting up organizations to represent diverse local values and interests was something that both groups did quite late in their efforts owing to perceived need for more legitimate forms of organization with "better" representation. This delay can be partly attributed to the great deal of uncertainty surrounding where their efforts were headed and what might eventually take form. For Denman, a sense of urgency, community factions, and vague goals and objectives definitely came into play; it took two and a half years after forming the buy-out sub-committee (DFI) to establish an official central organizing body. While there was long a small core group of people interested in forestry on Denman Island there was no pre-existing administration or organization (e.g. band council, municipality) to build on, other than the monitoring sub-committee (DFC) of the Ratepayers' Association. Owing to the low level of formal institutional development locally, the co-operative had to be conceived, agreed upon, and developed from nothing. Several Denman Island supporters noted that the ensuing logging added stress that forced community action before residents were really prepared:

> In all previous discussions with Hancock the issue of how the community was going to deal with [the community forest] and pay for it really wasn't addressed, because, you know [it's] a very difficult issue to get consensus on . . . to sit down around an issue so abstract. *Greg, Denman Island*

While the Denman organizers certainly demonstrated adaptive capabilities and perseverance, the overall process remained too unstructured, rushed and reactive to be effective:

> In the early stages we were just meeting as a group and just doing tasks as they came up. *Nelson, Denman Island*

Conversely, Cortes Island organizers had more time for planning, having initiated ecosystem-based management planning and community engagement processes nearly 7 years prior to making any formal purchase proposals to the company and province. In 1992, forestry consultants were hired and the community as a whole had already worked through many difficult questions by the time they received their plan in 1996. Several large community meetings provided a forum for community deliberation among individuals with different interests who, under other circumstances, might not usually have convened. Much time and internal community debate was necessary to reach some form of consensus as to the appropriate goals and objectives, management approach and organizational structure for the planned community forest on Cortes.

Once equipped with a vision for local control of the island's forest ecosystem, the Cortes Ecoforestry Society was formed in 1998. This level of organization gave the Klahoose–CES partnership a better bargaining position from the standpoint of having a well-developed set of plans, maps and formal organizational framework to support a credible working relationship.

MOTIVATIONS FOR LOCAL CONTROL: NATURAL RESOURCE AND AMENITY DEVELOPMENT PRESSURE

The most prevalent motivation for local control on both islands was to restrain the rate and extent of forest harvesting and residential development. In some respects Denman residents have more individual control (than in other communities) over what happens on their island because there is no local government presence. A network of volunteers manages Denman Island supported by a tradition of cooperatives. There is also no regular on-site law enforcement locally; police and Islands Trust by-law officers must come over by ferry from Vancouver Island. It is a quiet community where residents feel they are at arm's-length from off-island or "outside" influences. When Hancock initially resumed logging Denman residents were up in arms because of the sudden change imposed from outside. As one Denman representative shared:

> . . . the community reaction was to the logging. It wasn't so much the practices as the pace of logging which they'd proposed . . . the island hadn't seen that in 25 years. *Nelson, Denman Island*

As in the case of the Freedom Town Forest discussed in Chapter 3 of this book, Denman Islanders had long enjoyed free and open access to company forest lands and had an attachment to the lands as "common space" even though the land was privately owned. Under Hancock's ownership, things suddenly started moving too quickly for residents who were used to having more control over local events. The eventual choice of governance structure highlights local desires to uphold democracy, as emphasized by one community forest advocate:

> We decided to create it as a cooperative, not a society, or not a company, deliberately because we wanted a structure with more community control, or more secure community control. We were contemplating owning a large valuable asset, we didn't want to run the risk of it getting within the control of a small group of people. *Nelson, Denman Island*

The residents wanted to make sure that even a small group of locals could not control the destiny of the proposed community forest. Residents wanted the authority to decide what happened to the forests they lived in. Although the business plan included a component for local economic development, it was a secondary pursuit. The timber harvesting component would have made it possible to acquire and repay the loan. Residents were prepared to do some harvesting on the basis that they owned the land and could decide how it would proceed.

Cortes Island residents also resisted the control of large-scale forestry companies and logging practices that were deemed socially, economically and environmentally unsustainable. The impetus behind community monitoring efforts and eventual logging protests was decidedly environmental. However, interviews found more fundamental issues beneath the surface that related to power and value differentials between an isolated and independent island community and distant government and industry decision-making authorities:

> The community has to live with the results of whatever is done on the land base on Cortes and, therefore, I would say naturally, would like to be a player in making those decisions about how those activities are going to be carried out and what the end results are going to be like. *Edward, Cortes Island*

> [The Ministry of Forests] would come from "over seas" and bring their plans and tell us what was good for us. Similar things happened from even further afield with the Crown operators. The Crown District Manager is in Powell River as well. So it was all off-island and Cortes didn't like people from off-island telling *us* what *they* were going to do. *Vincent, Cortes Island*

In many respects the lack of local control over development and decision-making is part of the classic hinterland dilemma – though the lands and forests on Cortes and Denman are no longer perceived locally as a resource "storehouse." There has been much socio-cultural and economic transition over time so that these communities do not depend solely on resource extraction. First Nations and non-Aboriginals have been working to increase recognition for what they consider to be a homeland, with both groups demanding increased local involvement in local forestry and land-use planning. When asked about community motivations for a community forest, participants recognized economic and environmental opportunities, but the primary underlying motive was to gain control over and slow forest and land development.

On Cortes Island, concerns for development pressure were directly related to forest conservation and quality of life. Securing control of the forest company properties was important to community forest plans for economic and environmental reasons, as well as guarding against development by off-island purchasers seeking only to "log and flog" the land. There was perceived potential for further subdivision and development with each land sale from major holdings:

> You know, on a place like Cortes the pressure to convert the forest into residential use is high, and so every road that they built was a potential subdivision. *Gene, Cortes Island*

Cortes Island is attractive, and residents want to protect the island from rampant development that could have environmental, economic, and cultural implications. Many are very aware of the fact that continued logging on private lands could be followed by land sales, subdivisions and more people. In many respects, local control was a way to avoid unwanted changes to physical and human landscapes.

The push for a community forest on Denman Island was largely a response to steadily increasing development pressure. Residents were concerned about losing the forests but, as on Cortes, they appeared to be really concerned about how subsequent residential development would change social and local power relations, and the local cultural and economic setting more generally. Some voiced these concerns directly during interviews:

> People are afraid all the time that all these really ugly people are going to come, but I'm also afraid of what money and development [could do] because there's always going to be this push for development and jobs. We've had to fight them back on development, 'cause we don't want timeshare lodges. We wanna have our own little B and B, you know, hire our own people, *not* work for you thank you very much. *Joanne, Denman Island*

> My concern is it's going to change the character of the community. So you're gonna get a different sort of person here, and it's too sudden. What we're seeing on the island the last few years is the property values are just zooming like they are everywhere else. It's obviously going to force [current] people off the island. The taxes are going up and a lot of the houses being built now are million dollar houses. *Brian, Denman Island*

Residents were concerned about different values coming into the community with the influx of affluent people buying upscale housing. There were concerns that the island's economy would also continue to change with negative implications for locals. As evinced by the above comments, many held the perception that this transition was already under way, occurring too quickly, and that it was beyond local control. On Denman, securing ownership of forest company lands for a community forest was seen as a mechanism for controlling logging and "inevitable" development on a very large portion of the island. In the final analysis, residents of both islands wanted to be the ones who decided on the amount and type of development that might proceed.

CONCLUSION

As forest economies restructure, a "post-productivist landscape of consumption" is emerging in some former forest-dependent communities where new residents, values, lifestyles and economic pursuits are diverging from tradition (Gill and Reed 1999; Hanna 2005). In the island communities discussed above, significant changes occurred after decades of quiet inactivity on the Crown and private properties managed primarily by the major forest companies. With the past departure or reduction of timber harvesting, Denman and Cortes also decreased their dependence on forestry jobs (relative to other places in the province) and began transitioning to other opportunities in the tourism sector and tertiary and quaternary service delivery. Amenity migrants increasingly have moved in, leading to population growth at a rate twice that of the provincial average, causing demographic change, rising real-estate values and a further shift in local values. Middle-class newcomers often bring different visions and notions of rurality to more traditionally extractive forest resource settings that can lead to a tumultuous reimaging of place (Gill and Reed 1997). In the above cases, this shift has contributed to further support for, but also convolution of, ongoing local movements for local control to curb development.

The cases presented in this chapter show that the regenerating of forest properties held by absentee landowners, whether by the province or timber companies, has led them to become part of a different forest community landscape – one where ironic local trespassers and squatters regularly interact with "their forests" and monitor change. The fear for these and other forest communities is that large industry will eventually come back to formerly logged parcels as the timber matures, opening the door to further residential and tourism development on newly cleared lands. Under these circumstances, conflict appears certain. The above case studies point to the need to consider regulations for private forest lands; residents are otherwise compelled to take matters into their own hands. Conflict and change characterized local and provincial efforts to develop novel forest governance institutions, such as community forests, to enable local control.

Although these communities appear to be similar in terms of motivations, values and economies, their different patterns of land ownership, including the direct involvement of one local First Nation, and resulting local governance structures contributed to different events unfolding. (As previously outlined in Chapter 1 of this book, community forests are unique across local contexts even when numerous factors suggest homogeneity.) This is especially true with respect to the level of senior government involvement and support on Cortes versus Denman. Also important was the influence of returning private timber companies. These corporate "citizens" had profit motivations and development plans for their private holdings that quite clearly diverged from those of the island communities within which they were embedded. The forest companies had two objectives: (1) to profit by selling logs and (2) to profit from selling the logged-over land to developers. They were not based in the communities, had no interest in them and did not have to live next to the results of their activities. Event timing and the uncertainty of dealing with outside forest interests (i.e. government agencies and land owners) determined, to a large extent, how quickly Denman Islanders proceeded to later planning stages for strategic reasons. They also lacked the longer lead time prior to land transfer negotiations that Cortes Islanders had for gathering support, generating consensus, and developing plans and proposals. By slowing things down on Cortes, the involvement of First Nations and provincial governments also allowed the collective and planned mobilization of community resources. Although different organizational models were used to accommodate the various parties involved across settings, both communities pursued the development of more open, inclusive and representative decision-making structures for forest governance through the establishment of the Klahoose–Cortes Ecoforesty Society Partnership and the Denman Island Forest Cooperative.

At present, the contested forests discussed here are arguably more important to lifestyle and tourism than to direct jobs in forestry. Island ecology was also a big concern. Thus, local control was the primary motivation for community forestry, whether it was to have increased control over residential, commercial or industrial development. As each community sought to implement ecosystem-based forest management principles, they shared common values, though with varying degrees of emphasis. This reminds us of the diverse values to be represented in forest management at the community level all across the province of British Columbia (Bullock *et al.* 2009) and in other developed forest regions (see Chapters 3, 7 and 8). Yet above all, these case studies illustrate the transition of the BC forest industry, the changing community values and the way that the character of resource communities has increasingly changed from "hinterland" to "homeland." The relationship between forests and communities has evolved, and forest managers face new sets of challenges in managing human–environment interactions.

Reconciling differences in, or integrating, the perceptions, attitudes and values that shape our understanding of past and present conditions is critical to what is viewed as possible and acceptable for the future (Hanna and Slocombe 2007). Taking on paradigmatic challenges to implementation is paramount to achieving integration in forest ecosystem management (Behan 1990). As seen above, the provincial government and Ministry of Forests have tended to view community forestry as one way to stimulate local economies and, in certain settings, to mitigate conflict, rather than a way for locals to create more protected areas or constrain harvest levels. Communities with motivations that do not fit these economic intentions are less likely to succeed under evolving provincial frameworks. Policy makers and forest managers need to acknowledge that some communities are transitioning from resource to service economies with increasing populations and shifting values. Ecosystem-based management, a willingness to collaborate and to test out more representative and decentralized decision-making structures such as cooperatives and societies, and non-timber forest values are part of an evolving and new local institutional context that supports community forests. The success of community forestry depends on the extent to which governments can enhance the development of new visions and provide form to new but otherwise sound ideas. This in turn depends on an ability to identify and more objectively consider the underlying principles from which said "local" ideas evolved – from contexts of contestation and transition – rather than pass judgement on how things *should* proceed based on past experience with the mainstream.

NOTES

1 Akin to a county government.
2 Beginning in the mid 1980s, the BC government began to enact a series of statutes that have prohibited local governments from restricting forestry operations on managed forest lands through the adoption of by-laws or permitting (e.g. Private Forest Managed Land Act) (Islands Trust 2008: 3). The Islands Trust is currently seeking an exemption from the Act in order to gain more local control over private land management practices and development.
3 Not part of a municipality (village, town or city) or other local government, other than the Regional District.

REFERENCES

Beattie, D. (1997). Industrial forestry within a fragile island against its largest landowner. *The Voice*, October 1997: 4–11.
Behan, R. (1990). Multiresource forest management: A paradigmatic challenge to professional forestry. *Journal of Forestry* **88**(4): 12–18.
Bradley, T., Hoffman, J. and Hammond, H. (1998). *An Ecosystem-based Assessment of Denman Island*. British Columbia: Silva Ecosystem Consultants Ltd.
British Columbia Ministry of Environment (BCMOE) (2010). New Release: B.C. protects sensitive lands on Denman Island. Available at http://www2.news. gov.bc.ca/news_releases_2009-2013/2010ENV0062-001243.htm. Accessed January 10, 2012.

Bullock, R., Hanna, K. and Slocombe, S. (2009). Learning from community forestry experience: Challenges and lessons from British Columbia. *Forestry Chronicle* **85**(2): 293–304.

Cortes Ecoforestry Society (2002). *Cortes Community Forest Agreement Proposal, Draft.* Manson's Landing, Cortes Island, BC: Cortes Ecoforestry Society.

Cortes Ecoforestry Society (undated). *Summary.* Cortes Island, BC: Cortes Ecoforestry Society.

Denman Community Forest Cooperative (DCFC) (2001). *Denman Community Forest Cooperative homepage.* Available at http://www.denmanis.bc.ca/forestry.htm. Accessed March 1, 2005.

Gibson, C., E. Ostrom and Ahn, T. (2000). The concept of scale and the human dimensions of global change: A survey. *Ecological Economics* **32**: 217–39.

Gill, A. and Reed, M. (1997). The reimaging of a Canadian resource town: Post-productivism in a North American context. *Applied Geographic Studies* **1**(2): 129–47.

Gill, A. and Reed, M. (1999). Incorporating post-productivist values into sustainable community processes. In Pierce, J. and Dale, A. (eds.), *Communities, Development, and Sustainability across Canada*. Vancouver, BC: UBC Press.

Hanna, K. (2005). Planning for sustainability: Two contrasting communities. *Journal of the American Planning Association* **71**(1): 27–40.

Hanna, K. and Slocombe, D.S. (eds.) (2007). *Integrated Resource and Environmental Management: Concepts and Practice.* Don Mills, ON: Oxford University Press.

Islands Trust (2008). *Islands Trust Briefing on Private Managed Forest Land Act.* Available at http://www.islandstrust.bc.ca. Accessed July 1, 2011.

Islands Trust (2011). Islands Trust Council homepage. Available at http://www.islandstrust.bc.ca. Accessed July 1, 2011.

Jentoft, S. (2000). The community: A missing link of fisheries management. *Marine Policy* **24**: 53–9.

Klahoose First Nation, Cortes Ecoforestry Society, and Weyerhaeuser Company Ltd. (2000). *The Cortes Initiative: A Proposal to the Government of British Columbia.* A proposal prepared by the Klahoose First Nation, Cortes Ecoforestry Society, and Weyerhaeuser Company Limited.

Lemos, M. and Agrawal, A. (2006). Environmental governance. *Annual Review of Environment and Resources* **31**: 297–325.

Silva Forest Foundation (1996). *Initial Report on the Methodology and Results of Cortes Island Ecosystem Based Plan.* British Columbia, Canada: Silva Forest Foundation.

Statistics Canada (2006). *Community Profiles 2006.* Available at http://www12.statcan.gc.ca/census-recensement/2006/dp-pd/prof/92-591/index.cfm?Lang=E. Accessed July 1, 2011.

Statistics Canada (2001). *Community Profiles 2001.* Available at http://www12.statcan.ca/english/profil01/CP01/. Accessed July 1, 2011.

Watershed Sentinel (2011). Cortes Island Community Forest: Coming home. Available at http://www.watershedsentinel.ca/content/cortes-island-community-forest-coming-home. Accessed January 10, 2011.

7

The southwestern United States: community forestry as governance

This chapter was first subtitled *Community forestry as environmental governance*. As we worked though the history of community forestry in the American west, and looked into the case study literature, it became apparent that the word *environmental* might be limiting. In part this is because the term often carries the suggestion of preservation; the word can be more divisive than inclusive, which is unfortunate but nevertheless a reality. The definition of environmental governance, at least the one we hold out here, is based on the notion of inclusiveness manifest in processes that integrate diverse community values into decision-making about environmental resources – all with the intent of maintaining the integrity and resilience of natural systems that provide the basis for human wellbeing. A tall order to be sure. Such ideas are quite at home with fundamental notions of community forestry as a framework that respects the interdependence of forest landscapes and forest communities, and contains integrated objectives and strategies based on the equally important social, economic and ecological qualities of places (Baker and Kusel 2003; Wycoff-Baird 2005; Padgee *et al.* 2006). This "three-legged stool," as Baker and Kusel (2003) label it, is certainly akin to the three pillars of sustainability. Identifying the governance model that would actually implement the three-legged model is a trickier undertaking, but one many have attempted. It is often in these efforts that we see the fundamental differences in approaches to community forestry that emerge in different places.

The institutional and administrative contexts within which community forestry is implemented are highly variable, even within one nation such as the United States, and the ideal of community control, a common theme in community forestry discourses, may not be possible in many places unless there are significant, even radical changes to institutional structures. Such changes would also have to reflect the regional qualities that exist with the United States, despite the reality that the macro-institutions that manage public forest lands are in many respects homogenous and often distant from the locales and resources they govern. Non-homogenous regions governed by distant homogenous institutions: this is not exactly a good formula for responsive community resource management.

The movement in the western United States is not so much about changing the ownership of land, personified in different tenure arrangements, as it is about access to decision-making. It also reflects fundamental conflicts, ideological and intellectual, about the nature of a community's control over its own destiny, reflected in the capacity and power to determine the use of land. Burns (2003) writes in the opening to his case study of the Catron County, New Mexico, that the "story of the West is almost always about land – and its many forms and features: open range, water, timber, wilderness, cattle, mountains and mesas as far as the eye can see." A persuasive image, one that suggests that community forestry might really be an issue of environmental governance – and it is. Baker and Kusel (2003: 121) write that community forestry advocates and practitioners have been creating a new form of "Jeffersonian political practices" at the local and regional levels; but their words may be a bit hopeful. In recent years we have also seen interesting changes in the American political landscape, notably with the rise of the seemingly anti-government Tea Party movement. Governance is taking on a new meaning, but what this meaning is remains uncertain. This nascent political faction is potent, but driven by a harsh ideology that lacks cohesion, and it may be short-lived. If enacted to its fullest ideological extent, this movement would not only lessen and weaken regulatory enforcement, but also would be likely to gut the range of programs that support the diversification of forest-based communities.

As the US federal government struggles with the political–dogmatic mantra of "cost cutting," which runs the risk of being applied like an indiscriminate scythe, the effects on natural resources policy, and the management of National Forest and the US Forest Service in particular remain unclear. As we discuss here, however, community forestry, or the movements to which it has sometimes been connected, is varied in its objectives and approaches; they also reflect fundamental tensions within US society, not least of which is the relationship between resource-dependent, or land-dependent, communities and the senior levels of government and professionals (elites) that represent agencies and seem to make decisions in isolation from the needs and hopes of local people. Despite advances, governance, access to public lands and tenure remain fundamental understated issues, still essential to the success and progress of American community forestry (Christoffersen *et al.* 2008).

Community forestry in the American west is also about broader issues of governance, not just the "environment" and the limited landscape issues the term implies, but other, larger and more seemingly intractable economic, social and intuitional dynamics rooted in a belief that access to the resources provided by public lands is no longer equitable nor assured to local communities. And perhaps this reflects a grudging and implicit rejection of the reality of public land ownership. The current political climate and the new-found power of a radical Libertarian movement might be used, quite effectively if not correctly, to transform the role of federal agencies and the lands they administer, or to weaken them to the point that agencies are irrelevant and public lands are unregulated. The problem is that communities may be no better off, and may indeed end up in a worse state.

When we considered how best to approach a general discussion of community forestry in the US southwest the first instinct was to be broadly descriptive and provide an overview composed of small snippets (examples) of the application of community forestry. Some case studies stood out, but as with story genres some are more gripping than others. Then we remembered the June 1996 edition of *High Country News* – it featured Catron County, a place where economic decline and planning decisions over forestry land use had led to internecine conflict among community members and with federal agencies, notably the US Forest Service. It profiled not only the conflict, but also individuals at the center of it all. The story became widely known, and the County's approach to dealing with the US federal government, through country ordinances, became a bit of a *cause célèbre* among those in a growing movement that was quite actively advocating local control of federally "owned" lands. We give an account of events in Catron County here in part because the story is interesting and in some respects highlights the extremes that can come to the fore during economic and environmental changes, but also because it is a hopeful story with unique attributes that distinguish it from other examples from the American west. It is, as Baker and Kusel (2003: 128) state, among the best-known stories of community forestry on public lands where there has been innovation in community involvement and creative responses to seemingly obstinate, incapacitating and on some occasions violent confrontations about how public lands (that is to say local National Forests) should be managed. There are constant themes within community forestry that are well explored in this book, and innovation or at least the quest for it, successful or otherwise, is one of those constants.

While tenure in Canada may dominate the fundamental idea about what constitutes community forestry, in the western United States it is very much about communities being heard when decisions are made about how public forestlands will be used, who will benefit and how decisions will be made. Charnley and Poe (2007: 309) write that there has been a resistance to and lack of political support for giving communities tenure; such resistance comes largely from government agencies and environmental groups. Agencies feared the loss of budgets and power. Environmental groups feared the locals, and more specifically what they might do if left to run amok, chainsaws in hand, rapidly felling the last of America's old-growth forests.

If we put flippancy aside, certainly both government and environmental groups have honest concerns about the capacity and motives of some of those who advocate local control. What communities fear is the loss of jobs and decline in community economic stability. While legal constraints are important, there is also a pervasive belief that community control will cause forest degradation and that community-based management will favor local over national interests when making decisions about land use (Charnley and Poe 2007). This is not to say that tenure is not an issue in the southwestern United States, but rather that ideas about how to achieve inclusiveness are complex and often focused on "due" process, deliberative discourse, respect for traditional uses, and complex ideas about plurivocality rooted in history, culture and fear.

Wilson (2003) uses the term "collaborative stewardship" to describe community forestry in the southwestern United States. In this sense, community forestry issues are very much about a greater degree of community control, and not wholly or necessarily about ownership. The basic premise of community forestry in the United States and arguably elsewhere is that many forest-dependent communities are seeking a certain empowerment through effective participation in natural resource management policy and decision-making (Gray *et al.* 2001). The underlying theory is decentralization and devolution – where devolution implies a condition under which rights, responsibilities and discretionary authority (power) move from central government agencies to communities, while decentralization sees the transfer of administrative functions to lower branches of government (Charnley and Poe 2007). Putting either of these notions into practice has not been easy, despite widespread integration of collaborative stewardship, in various forms, into forest planning and management.

In addition to conflict, a range of institutional and governance limits to implementation must be overcome by most if not all community forestry settings. The success of implementation, as we have discussed elsewhere in this book, is setting-specific, and the difficulties can have context-specific features. Wilson (2003: 219–23) outlines five pervasive challenges to the implementation of community-based collaboration in the western United States:

1. Scale and public representation. National versus local scales confound management of national forests, where agencies exist within the context of a national government and must respond to national policy imperatives and pressures from national environmental organizations. These latter voices can conflict and work against locally defined goals and solutions. So, whose voice counts, and what is the role and power "of the local" when faced with well-organized pressure emanating from a greater scale?

2. Authority and the role of scientific knowledge. Capacity, marginalization and knowledge can be an issue when participation is expanded, but there is an expectation that scientific knowledge and expertise will remain core to considering management options and making decisions. This may require the education of participants, which runs the risk of becoming cooption, but also an openness to other forms of knowledge – forms that may be less scientific, but nevertheless potentially valid and innovative. The credibility of science may also be suspect. Some within a community will see its role as the legitimization of contentious practices, practices that may be at the root of conflicts; while others may see science employed to reduce resource use and change traditional land uses.

3. Translating public participation into policy. In the United States there are legal restrictions against interest groups serving as advisors for public land managers, which makes the direct role of such participation difficult to manage and account for. Part of the problem is the labeling of community organizations as special interests; however, as Wilson (2003) notes, the act of consultation and the influence of the resulting collaborative learning environment helps to shape decisions, without unduly influencing them. It is somewhat convoluted, but a legal reality nevertheless. More conceptually,

there are always challenges in integrating diverse perspectives and expectations into policy decisions, especially in light of the challenges noted above. And there is the expectation, on the part of those who participate in collaborative processes, that their opinions and the results of hard work will be recognizable in the outcomes.

4. Implementation and monitoring. As we discussed in Chapter 2, implementation, especially within conflict settings, is a particular challenge for community forestry since the basic premises of the concept can be at odds with the institutional setting and the capacities and cultures of implementing organizations. Monitoring, which in this context implies both a technical and policy performance perspective, requires consistency in participation and support. Since volunteerism is increasingly essential, capacity and regularity of participation can become problems, and transience in interest and membership poses risks to seeing projects through. As communities change, agreements may have to be rethought as the compacts developed among community members and managing agencies may not stand the test of time.

5. Adapting to place-specific contexts. The unique social and environmental qualities of places mean that a standardized community forestry model is unlikely to be practicable, but standardization is what is increasingly sought. Wilson (2003) links this to the influence of Progressive Era ideals. Success of community forestry will ultimately depend in no small part on acknowledgement of the unique qualities and expectation of places, and a uniform model is unlikely – that is to say, unlikely to work in all places.

The extent to which these challenges are present or significant varies depending on the setting, and several aspects (notably the legal restrictions on the influence of participation) are unique to the American context. Wilson's list is helpful for characterizing challenges and for developing implementation frameworks, and it is specific to the western American experience. He also uses the phrase "community-based collaboration" to frame his approach. This is not necessarily the same as community forestry *per se*, at least as it is defined in other locales. Wilson (2003: 219) notes that by some counts over 90% of national forests are engaged in some form of community collaboration; the same cannot be said of exactingly defined community forestry models where community control and/or tenure assignment are present, and these are certainly much fewer in number in the American case. If anything, this means that defining what constitutes community forestry, especially in the western United States, certainly has to be adaptive and perhaps somewhat solutive.

We know that community forestry also dwells uncomfortably within the realm of discourse about addressing pervasive conflicts between forest management bureaucracies and the people whose livelihoods are forest-dependent. Conflict flows in part from the increasing complexity of forest-dependent communities reflected in new economies, economic decline, new people, new ideas and perceptions of nature and land use, and the seemingly perpetual quest for community resilience – social and economic – that is regularly phrased as the pursuit of sustainability. Conflict also flows from a feeling of powerlessness, exacerbated by economic decline, and gradual realization that economic and social change is occurring and may not be thwarted, certainly in the long term. The issues are multifaceted and intertwine history, class, race, regional identity, environmentalism and economics. Social stability may also be based on a civil society that demands conformity (Swanson 2001). The decline of economic opportunity coupled with the introduction of new people and new ideas fractures social orthodoxy, and exacerbates the potential for conflict. The social stability of communities, based on an established interaction with the land, suddenly seems unsustainable. This causes an uncomfortable reflection where blame is assigned to governments, notably the federal government, and the dream of local control, or in the case here "county control," seems a panacea. Regardless, the emergence of community forestry in the American west has been stirred by the policy stalemate that results from passionate "interest group" battles at the national level, due in no small part to the concentration of power within national institutions that operate in an adversarial way through legislation and the judicial remedy (Gray *et al.* 2001; Moote *et al.* 2001; Johnson *et al.* 2001). It can seem that some communities have only the most reactive and unconsidered responses to decline and its causes, but in reality community understanding, the responses and the reasons for them, and their articulation of potential and realized solutions are often sophisticated and poignant.

The community forestry movement in the US west reflects a visceral concern on the part of communities about the flow and retention of wealth from local forest resources. Baker and Kusel (2003: 9) write that the investment is a central theme in community forestry – where investment is seen in terms as the flow of value from forest ecosystems and thus from the communities that rely on them. In this vein, new approaches, based on community needs, are integrative, and inherently linked to equity, social justice and the health of ecosystems from which community wealth flows. McDermott (2009a, 2009b) analyzes power relations under community forestry. The assertion is that community forestry can help bring about social change if it alters who has access to natural resources and who makes decisions (McDermott 2009a). Baker and Kusel (2003) link the community forestry movement to the often-cited core themes of sustainability (economy, society and nature) and present it as something that gives sustainability an applied flavor, something quite different from its oft-perceived ethereal qualities. In the United States as a whole, community forestry initiatives have tended to rely on collaborative ventures between managing agencies and community organizations to achieve conservation and restoration of forest ecosystems and ultimately to sustain forest communities (Charnley and Poe 2007; Baker and Kusel 2003; Gray *et al.* 2001).

The antecedents of the most recent community forestry movement are rooted in the institutional leavings of the conservation era. The conservation movement, which greatly shaped land ownership in the American west, emerged in the late 1800s and was an ascendant, though much debated, force in US public policy. Its impacts are lasting. Beyond its well-understood impact on resource use and tenure, the movement spawned among other things public utilities, expansion of the national parks system, and the still powerful anti-trust legislation. All were guided by a sense of equity in access to opportunity and the vast resources that were foremost in the public imagination of what was the American west; but it was a western landscape that was quickly changing.

Arguably the basic tenets of public ownership, science-based management and the importance and power of professional resource management bureaucracies, key products of the Conservation Era (or the Progressive Era as some term it, e.g. Wilson 2003), remain central themes in American natural resource management today. In Theodore Roosevelt as President and Gifford Pinchot as the first head of the US Forest Service the movement had its greatest champions, and the lasting great profile of public lands and the importance of large federal agencies owes much to them. One need only look at a map of the American west to see this magnified federal presence represented in National Forests, National Parks, Indian reserves, military lands, vast reserves of various forms, and vast areas managed, or mismanaged, by the Bureau of Land Management and a myriad of other federal agencies (White 1997). This legacy helped set the stage for the conflictual and institutional context within which community forestry has emerged in the United States.

While Roosevelt and Pinchot may have envisioned a utilitarian ethic that guides land-use planning to meet the "greatest good for the greatest number," to paraphrase Pinchot, many communities see management as serving something else. That "something else" is not uncommonly perceived as alternatively being corporate interests or environmentalism – interests seen as unattached to communities, uncaring for employment and, in the instance of corporate welfare, a willingness to sacrifice the "sustainability" of communities and renewable resources for the sake of short-term profits. Such perceptions are not wholly accurate, but nor are they entirely inaccurate. And many innovative efforts are being tried, but the federal government still holds decision-making authority for federal forests. The delegation of power to communities to manage federal forests has rarely happened, and is indeed institutionally difficult to arrange (Charnley and Poe 2007). From our perspective, admittedly as outsiders, the essential fact in understanding the narrative of community forestry in the American west is that the great majority of productive forest land is owned by the US federal government.

A BRIEF HISTORY

The long-held perception that Aboriginal peoples in North America lived harmoniously with nature is often repeated in descriptions of the pre-European American west. Baker and Kusel (2003) note that Native American land-use practices had great capacity to alter forested areas, for example through burning which reduced forest cover and created more open "park-like" conditions. Hunting and gathering practices also change forests at a range of scales. It is also suggested that the cessation of indigenous practices, with the advance of European settlement, led to the decline of ecosystems that had in essence been maintained or created by Aboriginal peoples (e.g. Blackburn and Anderson 1993; Baker and Kusel 2003). The impact of Aboriginal peoples on forest lands has also been presented as being complex – that is to say, not always benign. Far from simply existing within forest landscapes, they actively exploited and changed them to something that became the "pristine" landscape that Europeans and later eastern Americans came to romanticize, an image given life in paintings by the likes of George Catlin, Paul Kane and Albert Bierstadt (see Krech 1999). Regardless of the impacts, many early peoples in the American west were very much tied to their forests as the place for provisions and for overt and subtler cultural underpinnings.

The initial settlement of the southwest by Spanish colonists created what may be the earliest forms of communal forest management in the American west, outside of Aboriginal communities. Common lands were established for grazing, timber and game, based on Spanish law and traditions and advanced to encourage Spanish settlement (Carlson 1990; Baker and Kusel 2003). By the mid twentieth century most of these common areas had been transformed from communal to private forms of ownership (Carlson 1990). Tax assessment policies also weakened communal ownership. As the US federal government gradually assumed control over larger areas of formerly communal forest lands, the role of US Forest Service grew and restrictions on customary uses ensued; this became the main factor in the emergence of a community forestry movement in the US southwest (Baker and Kusel, 2003).

The role of the Forest Service in the southwest and other regions is complex and shifting. The assumption that it has been mostly a champion of timber production is no longer accurate. With the growing power of divergent and notably non-industrial perspectives on land use, the Forest Service has had to alter its approaches and forest manage-ment plans. There has been extensive acceptance of increasing public participation in federal forest management, in part through collabora-tive mechanisms and as part of "the trend toward democratizing envir-onmental decision-making" that has evolved since the 1970s, and is notably apparent in the 2005 Forest Planning Rules (Charnley and Poe 2007: 309). As we noted above, by some measures, over 90% of US national forests were occupied with some form of collaborative stewardship as part of the management approach – an encouraging number (Wilson 2003: 219). Nevertheless, while the agency has been somewhat responsive to new expectations, it has not been entirely comfortable with change. Indeed, far from emerging solely from within the Forest Service the new paradigms in Forest Service planning have been a response to legislation and political ideological dictates. Initia-tives such as the New Perspectives program, which sought to implement ecosystem-based management, were alternatively praised as balanced and giving voice to non-industrial users within Forest Service decision-making (e.g. Salwasser 1991) and disparaged as a continuation of the agency's pro-commodity bias (e.g. Lawrence and Murphy 1992).

Regardless of the extent to which new paradigms radically change the Forest Service's culture, they have broadened perspectives, while the interpretation of a "new perspective" has likely been variable within the agency.

Although the US Forest Service has undergone some cultural changes, and there is debate about how powerful and meaningful these really are, what remains certain is that the fundamental institutional setting, embodied in law and tenure, is largely unchanged. Many will disagree with this, and that's fine, but decision-making remains formally in the bailiwick of the Forest Service, and in the United States there have been no substantive or extensive efforts to allocate tenure to community-based organizations. Unless there is a significant change in the way National Forests are legally defined, community control cannot happen. Such change seems unlikely, though it is not impossible. At best, what most communities can hope for is some form of consequential collaborative management, but even achieving that can be difficult. More realistically what can be accomplished is "enhanced communication," a state of being where structures are put in place so that communities and public land managers can communicate, understand each other's needs, sort through the administrative realities and hopefully enact change though formal and informal discourse.

A STORY FROM THE US SOUTHWEST

In the mid 1980s in the state of New Mexico, the US Forest Service management plan for the Gila National Forest responded to the Endangered Species Act in order to protect the Mexican spotted owl, but this led to a marked reduction in the timber program (Burns 2003). The decline in available timber, coupled with other economic factors, led to an economic downturn evident in the loss of logging and wood-processing jobs in Catron County, and the concurrent loss of management capacity in the Forest Service. As Burns (2003: 92) notes, the decline of the timber program saw a reduction in the number of Forest Service silviculturalists, ecologists and sales-administrators, which eventually meant that the agency could not carry out its own management objectives. Gila National Forest was essentially shut down (McDermott 2009a). The region came to exemplify the conflicts between logging and ranching – the long-time land users – and environmentalism. It is hard to say that new people were wholly responsible for bringing forth new perspectives; land degradation issues were longstanding but had simmered rather than coming to the fore. The emergence of new views pitted "traditional" uses, characterized as ranching and logging, against other uses – uses that are less extractive.

Conflict at this time was not limited to places like Catron County, or its southern neighbor Grant County, but was part of what Burns (2003: 93) describes as a "contentious rhetoric [that] swept the west as the environmental movement and rural community economies clashed in ideological confrontation." This would spawn catchphrases and movements such as Earth First, Wise Use, "custom and culture," private property rights movements, county sovereignty and the "County Supremacy Movement" (Burns 2003; McCarthy 2002; Miller 1993, 1994, 1995). These monikers came to represent a call for community control over local resources. Of course, who should control these and for what values they should be managed would prove problematic and as conflictual as the perceived distance of the federal government.

In his 1996 article for the *High Country News*, Davis portrayed the gradual rise in acrimony that accompanied the decline of the timber and ranching economies and the new management approaches on of the Forest Service – approaches that emphasized the scaling back of logging and efforts to protect riparian and range resources. The latter would have impacts on long-established grazing practices. In response, the Catron County government developed what Davis (1996) describes as an anti-federal blueprint, where county officials harkened back to the speeches of the Founding Fathers, to the US Constitution, to constitutional amendments protecting individual rights, to the US Civil Rights Act, and to long ago Spanish and Mexican customs. The rhetoric was followed by the passing of county ordinances – no wolves, mountain lions or bears could be released into the wild; the county government must consent or at least be consulted before federal agencies could regulate the use of public land; grazing on public land was defined as a private property right; and private property rights were defined as civil rights (Davis 1996). By endeavoring to declare sovereignty over the federal lands within its boundaries, the Catron County government was now in effect spearheading the budding County Supremacy Movement (McCarthy 2002; Wilson 2006). Legal skirmishes ensued – testing the definition of private property, what constitutes property rights, rights of access to public lands, and the need for Environmental Impact Statements when the Forest Service designated critical habitats (see Miller 1995; Bertelson 1996). In due course the County's approach failed to withstand court rulings, but the genuine effort symbolized local grievances with federal land management, and awareness and frustration over the powerlessness of communities to shape the nature of economic change (Wilson 2006).

Regardless of legal setbacks, a political movement was now well under way. Davis (1996) writes:

> The county's message had been clear: get the federal government out of people's lives. The county can do a better job in managing national forests and other public land than any federal bureaucrat. Any federal action that diminishes the value of public land's use – ranching, logging and mining – is a 'taking' requiring financial compensation.

As conflict grew, the County gained a reputation among some as "the model for community control" and resistance to federal land management decisions that impacted local economies by restricting resource access, while in other quarters the County was seen as a place of extreme views. Journalists took note. It was attention that was not entirely welcome. While some County officials were loath to see themselves branded as "county supremacists," a label that was in their eyes incorrect and symbolic of a media message controlled by government officials and "outsiders" (Burns 2003: 95), others openly spoke of confrontation with the federal government: "rebellion . . . if things don't change" (Chaloupka 1996: 164). And some of the comments from local politicians seemed eccentric. The Catron County Attorney, writing in the *Hatch Courier*, a New Mexico weekly newspaper, said:

> . . . imagine, having 50 American republics instead of 50 states, each with a government tailored to the local cultures. New York State could be home for gay rights and gun control advocates. Utah could have polygamy. Eco-preservationists could govern Florida, and loggers could plant and chop trees in Oregon . . . (as quoted in Davis 1996)

The same official situated his actions and rhetoric in terms of a racial frontier, while making links between stories of Celtic rebellion and the US federal governments' protection of owls and fish over humans (White 1997). Helvarg (1999: 446) notes that soon after the first ordinances were passed, some county officials seemed to be encouraging the formation of a militia. One County Commissioner is quoted as stating, "Citizens are tired of being tossed around and pushed to the limit by regulations. We want the Forest Service to know we're prepared, even though violence would be a last resort" (Helvarg 1999: 446). At one point the Catron County Sherriff threatened to arrest the head of the US Forest Service (Chaloupka 1996: 165).

To a great extent, this all reflected a loathing of the federal government, born from the political and social evolution of part of the American west that tolerates little if any government interference (especially from the federal government), and prizes the myth of individualism, but at the same time has benefited greatly from federal encouragement and financial subsidies of programs and policies that help spur what western communities seem to crave the most: growth (White 1997). Things are quieter today, but such feelings may still run wide and just below the surface of a restored community civility.

If we remove the severe perspectives (i.e. the "outliers"), it appears that the mainstream search was for a different approach to governance – one that offered a modicum of power over place. Rather than "supremacy over federal lands" what was perhaps being sought by the broader community was a local role in planning for public lands, and consequential participation in decision-making processes that increasingly appeared to be dominated by what was viewed as an "extreme environmental position" outnumbering local voices (Burns 2003: 95). But the conflict was news in no small part because there was a whiff of old west violence as viewpoints collided, trust was lost, and coercion replaced the place of mutual discovery and community conversation (Burns 2003).

While conflict in Catron County began as a debate over forest resource management, it became a social crisis manifest in higher rates of alcohol use and spousal abuse, depression and a sense of loss of control over individual lives and choices (Burns 2003). Violence was an undertone, present and threatened, and as Helvarg (1999) recounts, not only the substance of utterances but at times seemingly next door. It appeared that all, regardless of their allegiances, felt the stress. It was within this setting that a community group was formed as part of a broader counseling effort and to help create a setting within in which even if broader forest and environmental management issues could not be settled conclusively, then at least a sense of civil society might be restored. The *Catron County Citizens' Group* was initiated from within the community and created with the help of medical professionals (who were seeing first hand the toll that conflict was taking on the health of the community) and dispute resolution experts. It would in short time also include broad representation from all levels of government, and non-government organizations representing multi-sectoral interests. Support from philanthropic foundations made the conflict resolution process possible.

To begin with, the Citizens' Group emphasized dialogue aimed at finding common ground in the pursuit of what was termed "an economic, social and environmentally sound future for local communities" (Wilson 2006: 64). This differentiates the Catron example from others in the west. The Citizens' Group sees its primary goal as "cultivating community cohesion and stability" by encouraging mediation of local conflicts and promoting economic development "through community-based restoration forestry projects on the Gila and Apache National Forests" (Wilson 2006: 63). Toward this end, the Group formed five working committees (Burns 2003: 98–99):

1. Education, which aimed to establish a social learning context, where sectoral interests learned about each other's needs, values and objectives, and a broader public education function to explain issues and conflict sources.
2. Dispute resolution, centred on developing processes for resolving differences and diffusing the emerging threat of violence.
3. Land stewardship, to find areas of agreement for maintaining and enhancing range and other environmental qualities.
4. Economic development, which emphasized diversification and new sources of economic opportunity.
5. Youth development, to encourage youth participation in the process and to create a sense of opportunity and hope.

At the earliest stages of the formation of the Citizens' Group, grazing (range) issues were the first test. Range management had long formed a significant part of the conflict setting. Forest Service actions to support ecological restoration or grazing areas had meant that in some areas the number of cattle permitted would have to be reduced. There were also pressures from environmentalists to reduce grazing. A mediation committee was formed, based on the belief that such conflicts had mostly to do with interpersonal issues, specifically different views, attitudes and backgrounds (Burns 2003: 102–3). While the efforts were seen as successful in improving interpersonal concerns, it is hard to say whether substantive changes in grazing policy were realized; rather, a better understanding and a more responsive approach to policy implementation seems to have been the real product. Indeed, as Burns (2003) relates, a pivotal conflict over range use was finally settled by the courts, and in this respect the timeliness of mediation aimed at improving the interpersonal setting may have much to do with success – it needs to be in place before conflict escalates.

The Citizens' Group facilitated dialogue about salvage log sales and restoration projects, which would seemingly be uncontroversial, but that was not the case. In most instances, where logging was proposed, debate ensued. Although the Citizens' Group facilitated the "discovery" of potential new opportunities for forest-based activities, decision-making still resided with the Forest Service. In the instance of a salvage timber sale, which culminated in a permit that had been the result of deep discussion and negotiation, the final accord (a local decision) was overruled by a US Department of Agriculture Undersecretary, effectively cancelling the salvage sale, and underscoring the belief that communities and local Forest Service offices would not really be allowed to develop effective collaborative initiatives (Burns 2003).

Regardless of such setbacks, and they are common in community forestry, the Citizens' Group continued its work and gradually moved into a project stage. Along with the County government and federal funding from the Collaborative Forest Restoration Program, the Group worked to purchase and reopen a closed mill yard. The objective was to establish a working site where wood could be held and sorted to support small-scale processing. The facility provides the space, infrastructure and equipment that small-scale wood manufacturers or processors would not readily have or necessarily afford.

At first glance the accomplishments of the Citizens' Group seem modest. Wilson (2006: 64) writes that perhaps the most interesting facet of the Citizens' Groups work with local residents is their support for a "youth conservation corps program," an initiative through which young people learn about forest ecology and gain skills in restoration forestry and practices that will ideally lead to employment in the local area. Further, by building linkages that reinforce of place-based and common socio-economic experience amongst young people, the program enhances and helps build new underpinnings for social cohesion (Wilson 2006). Burns (2003: 99) notes that some members of the Citizens' Group are a bit more considered in characterizing their success, commenting that success is measured in part as "We're still here" and "No one's gotten hurt." Success might be viewed in terms of scale and change to the social and communicative conditions that preceded conflict. The Group supported initiatives that in turn encouraged small processing and production ventures based on wood, but it also emphasized communication and provided a setting within which the trading of ideas, concerns and knowledge could occur. While there has been an emphasis on the outcomes of community forestry as being a model of management that balances social, economic and ecological dimensions equally (the "three-legged stool"), in practice this can be not only difficult to achieve within the institutional setting, but even difficult to define. Just like sustainability, its ideological twin, its definition is subjective and very much shaped by the individuals or organizations that use it.

McDermott (2009a) suggests a causal analysis as an alternative to the descriptive outcomes approach that seems more common in evaluating the success of community forestry. Such a framework focuses on the social drivers of change that produce outcomes, rather than figurative outcomes themselves; thus if community forestry increases local access to decision-making by changing power relationships then it will also bring about social transformation (McDermott 2009a). This emphasis on the social process of community forestry as the producer of community conditions also reminds us of the need to acknowledge a pervasive issue in community-based approaches: that is, that they may serve to reinforce existing power relationships and hierarchies rather than lead to a more equitable distribution of decision-making power and benefits (Charnley and Poe 2007).

The Catron County case presents characteristics common in the western United States. Declining economic and timber supply conditions preceded community forestry efforts, and it is a story that is conflict-based, albeit an extreme one. But it also has an important and unique quality. As Wilson (2006: 64) notes, the Citizens' Group in Catron is distinctive, compared with other community forestry examples in the American west, in the socio-cultural and political diversity of its membership. From the beginning there was an embracing of inclusiveness. In contrast, the Catron County experience is different from that of neighboring Grant County. Though Grant too had experienced significant decline in the timber economy and was also reliant on Gila National Forest, the community response took a different organizational tack. As McDermott (2009a: 255) relates, in Grant County the formation of a Jobs and Biodiversity Coalition (JBC), which also came together under polarized conditions and was formed with participation by diverse people, evolved into a closed process, albeit one that is "exclusively local". This is a modified form of a participation-limited model (Kusel et al. 1996). Meetings were open to all, but were never advertised. As in Catron County, the achievements are also small in scale: the creation of new small timber-based businesses, and a modest number of jobs. The Grant County example also included a role for collaborative community-based ecological monitoring, an activity that is seen as helping to build trust and foster social capital (Fernandez-Gimenez *et al.* 2008). Such achievements are significant in the context of limited economic opportunities and low potential for diversification. McDermott (2009a) writes that the main reason for the success of the JCB is indeed its narrow base. This base derived from an exclusivity rooted in locality that provided fundamental knowledge of place. The JCB includes the Forest Service and advocacy groups, and there is a willingness to make focused long-term commitments to participation. Exclusivity, it is suggested, in turn led to a productive relationship between community organizations and the Forest Service.

The Catron experience seems more complex and maybe messier. That process was quite open and inclusive, perhaps giving it greater potential in the long term to address persistent issues of social and economic inequality, which can permeate resource dependent communities. McDermott (2009a) suggests that while the "equity leg" is shorter than the others in the Grant County case, the JCB expanded resource access and created a new "decision-space," but it is arguable that the very qualities that made it successful in these efforts – a single-minded focus on forest restoration and value added activities – also make the exclusive model unsuitable for dealing with broader challenges in social inequity (McDermott 2009a: 258). The closed system has advantages, but it ultimately relies on a core group, often small in numbers, which may or may not be resilient. Organization success in a closed system and its survival are possibly more personality-dependent than would be the case in a broader, more inclusive model. Having said all this, as McDermott also notes, once even such a limited structure has been created there is the prospective of developing a more inclusive base, if that is permitted or demanded. To do this, however, such an organization will have to be locally based, possess credibility and show success that directly affects the well-being of the community, even if in a very limited sense.

ACCOMPLISHMENTS AND LIMITS

The implementation of community forestry in the southwestern United States is shaped in large part by the nature of public land ownership – and this is mostly federal. The compact between government(s), industry and communities was strong and stable, until economic conditions changed. The reasons for these changes are varied, but timber supply, the quality of business management, and changes in production processes and competition all played a role. Added to this mix was the emergence of a powerful, and often remote, environmental movement which increasingly sought to change forest management and harvesting practices radically or to shut down the industry all together. With these coming together at the same time, a "perfect storm" emerged. The result was the decline in local communities and – in many locales – conflict. The story is a common one, not just in Catron Country, but across the US west.

In Catron County the turn to community forestry was a reactive approach. It comes to the fore when conflict over access to forest resources emerges, when the compact between community, industry and government breaks down. Community forestry has as its strongest ideal the basic notion of community control, where tenure, or something very close to it, is vested in a community-based organization. A lesser version would be co-management in some form, but even this may be difficult within a legal setting that may relegate community organizations to the place of special interests. The Catron story illustrates what appears to be a common definition of success in community forestry; the achievements may seem quite small, especially when compared with the significant economic declines many communities have experienced. A few jobs may be created in new value-added businesses or small-scale harvesting, better access to salvage timber can be provided, and restoration or conservation programs supported. These opportunities are symbolic of change, and with time they may lead to larger enterprises and a greater degree of community control. We suggest that what also commonly emerges is "enhanced communication." What is difficult to measure is the significance or impact of facilitating dialogue; and this may be the most important immediate success of what is in essence a tenure-less community forestry model. In places where conflict looms large, and threatens even violence, such a community forestry model may provide the setting within which understanding is generated. There may be very real limits imposed by the institutional structure and social context of public landownership, and prescribed authority may be absent from the process; however this does not mean that it is without influence. Perhaps this is what happens when people in a community come together to talk about their values, needs and where they are "coming from," and ultimately seek common ground. Even in the absence of a formal mechanism for community control, a community-based process may obtain a certain power, albeit a reified one where the initiative can come to possess more informal power than formal authority.

REFERENCES

Baker, M. and Kusel, J. (2003). *Community Forestry in the United States*. Washington DC: Island Press.

Bertelson, R. (1996). Danger for the Endangered Species Act: Catron County Board of Commissioners, New Mexico v. United States Fish and Wildlife Service. *Journal of Natural Resources & Environmental Law* **12**: 167.

Blackburn, T. and Anderson, K. (eds.) (1993). *Before the Wilderness*. Menlo Park, CA: Ballena Press.

Burns, S. (2003). Catron County, New Mexico: Mirroring the West, healing the land, rebuilding community. In Kusel, J. and Adler, E. (eds.), *Forest Communities, Community Forests*. Lanham, MD: Rowman and Littlefield.

Carlson, A. (1990). *The Spanish-American Homeland: Four Centuries in Mexico's Rio Arriba*. Baltimore, MD: Johns Hopkins University Press.

Chaloupka, W. (1996). The County Supremacy and Militia Movements: Federalism as an issue on the radical right. *Publius* **26**(3): 161–75.

Charnley, S. and Poe, M.R. (2007). Community forestry in theory and practice: Where are we now? *Annual Review of Anthropology* **36**: 301–36.

Christoffersen, N., Don, L., Martha, W. and Wyckoff, B. (2008). Status of community-based forestry in the United States. In *A Report to the US Endowment for Forestry and Communities*. Greenville, SC: US Endowment.

Davis, T. (1996). Catron County's politics heat up as its land goes bankrupt. *High Country News*, June 26.

Fernandez-Gimenez, M.E., Ballard, H. and Sturtevant, V. (2008). Adaptive management and social learning in collaborative and community-based monitoring: A study of five community-based forestry organizations in the western USA. *Ecology and Society* **13**(2): 4.

Gray, G.J., Enzer, M.J. and Kusel, J. (eds.) (2001). *Understanding Community-Based Ecosystem Management in the United States*. New York: Hawthorn Press.

Helvarg, D. (1999). The anti-enviro connection. In Dizard, J., Muth, R. and Andrews, S. Jr (eds.), *Guns in America: A Reader*. New York: New York University Press.

Johnson, N.H., Ravnborg, M., Westermann, O. and Probst, K. (2001). User participation in watershed management and research. *Water Policy* **3**: 507–20.

Krech, S. (1999). *The Ecological Indian: Myth and History*. New York: W.W. Norton.

Kusel, J., Doak, S., Carpenter, S. and Sturtevant, V. (1996). *The Role of the Public in Adaptive Ecosystem Management, Sierra Nevada Ecosystem Project: Final report to Congress*, Vol II. *Assessment and Scientific Basis for Management Options*. Davis, CA: University of California, Davis, Centres for Water and Wildland Resources.

Lawrence, N. and Murphy, D. (1992). New perspectives or old priorities? *Conservation Biology* **6**: 465.

McCarthy, J. (2002). First World political ecology: Lessons from the Wise Use movement. *Environment and Planning A* **34**(7): 1281–302.

McDermott, M. (2009a). Locating benefits, expanding decision-spaces, resource access and equity in U.S. community-based forestry. *Geoforum* **40**(2): 249–59.

McDermott, M. (2009b). Equity first or later? How US community-based forestry distributes benefits. *International Forestry Review* **11**(2): 207–20.

Miller, A. (1993). All is not quiet on the Western Front. *Urban Lawyer* **25**: 827–40.

Miller, A. (1994). Western Front revisited. *Urban Lawyer* **26**: 845–57.

Miller, A. (1995). Private rights in public lands: The battle intensifies. *Urban Lawyer* **27**: 889.

Moote, M., Brown, B., Kingsley, E. *et al*, (2001). Process: Redefining relationships. *Journal of Sustainable Forestry* **12**: 97–116.

Padgee, A., Kim, Y. and Daugherty, P. (2006). What makes community forest management successful? A meta-study from community forests throughout the world. *Society and Natural Resources* **19**: 33–52.

Salwasser, H. (1991). New perspectives for sustaining diversity in US National Forest Ecosystems. *Conservation Biology* **5**: 567–69.

Swanson, L. (2001). Rural policy and direct local participation: Democracy, inclusiveness, collective agency and locality-based policy. *Rural Sociology* **66**(1): 1–21.

Walker, G. (2001). Process: Redefining relationships. In Gray, G., Enzer, M. and Kusel, J. (eds.) *Understanding Community Based Forest Ecosystem Management*. Binghamton, NY: Food Products Press.

White, R. (1997). The current weirdness in the West. *The Western Historical Quarterly* **28**(1): 4–16.

Wilson, R. (2003). Community-based management and national forests in the western United States: Five challenges. *Policy Matters* **12**: 216–24.

Wilson, R. (2006). Collaboration in context: Rural change and community forestry in the four corners. *Society and Natural Resources* **19**(1): 53–70.

Wyckoff-Baird, B. (2005). *Growth Rings: Communities and Trees, Lessons from the Ford Foundation Community-Based Forestry Demonstration Program, 2000–2005*. Washington, DC: The Aspen Institute.

8

Community access and the culture of stewardship in Finland and Sweden

When we reflect on experiences in the North American setting, it seems that one of the more understated objectives of community forest advocates is the actual fostering of a culture of forest stewardship. Undoubtedly such visions exist in North America, but they are becoming difficult to sustain as the role of the forest industries declines and populations become increasingly urban-based. In Finland and Sweden a strong cultural attachment to forests and the resources they provide has remained in place despite similar patterns of urbanization. However, in spite of a long history of permitting community access to forested lands, neither country has always encouraged public participation in forestry policy and planning processes. But the policy setting has evolved in recent years, and in no small part as a response to rising public concern about the state of forest management. The Finnish and Swedish experience begs a different interpretation of what "community forestry" is; one that makes us think about tenure and stewardship in different ways. It also highlights the important social processes at the local level that help to shape land-use policy and facilitate successful implementation (Folke *et al.* 2005; Schultz *et al.* 2007). Ownership, while important, does not negate the potential for developing community–forest interactions or a social sense of possession and accountability. Here, we outline some of the features and recent changes in forest policy in each nation and connect these transformations to the broad notion of community expectations, an enveloping theme in the larger community forestry dialogue. By contrasting the Scandinavian case with those from North America (Chapters 3 to 7 in this book), we reflect on whether "community forestry" can be claimed in instances where a forest stewardship is engrained in national culture.

The literal translation of the Finnish term *jokamiehenoikeus* and its Swedish equivalent *allemansrätten* is *(the) everyman's right*. The terms are

Figure 8.1 A managed forest in eastern Finland. In Finland most woodlands are intensively managed and are much altered forest systems. They bear little resemblance to the natural or "extensively" managed forests that dominated the country long ago. Whilst such landscapes have been long accepted, in recent years they have become a source of conflict as social values change and communities seek a more complex approach to forest management and forestry practices (photo: K. Hanna).

more commonly (and gender neutrally) defined as "common rights," "right of public access" or "the right to roam." This right of access applies to both public and private lands, and it arguably forms the basis of broad community use of forested lands (see Figure 8.1). It helps define the interaction of communities and individuals with forested lands and the benefits they provide. With some very old exceptions in the American northeast, private forest lands in many parts of North America limit public access. This was a feature seen as necessary to providing the foundation for settlement, investment, wealth creation and wealth retention. In contrast, the Scandinavian view of private forests is more nuanced and includes a very old provision for reasonable access. We say reasonable because access is not treated under contemporary law or by historic rules as the unfettered right to use forest resources as one pleases. There are rules, although these are defined by convention rather than strictly by law. What it does is allow the use of modest resources (e.g. mushrooms, berries, camping, and access or passage), activities that have become part of the consciousness of land – "space or place" if you want – of most of Scandinavia.

The institution of the everyman's right has old origins; indeed the concept was reflected in provincial laws and customs dating to the Middle Ages. Traces of the concept can be found elsewhere in Europe. In Britain, for example, elements of the right to roam inform the relatively new community forestry movement (Lawrence *et al.* 2009), and "rambling" across variably owned lands remains a "relative" right, but resource use is greatly restricted. The fact that it has not been greatly weakened in Sweden and Finland, as it was elsewhere in Europe, is perhaps owing to the absence of a feudal period, which in other countries led to a more unconditional sense of land and property ownership and a determined retention of the benefits that flow from land. And as time progressed these benefits increasingly accrued to a few, and legal structures grew to restrict community access. Some would argue that a strong sense of individualism also made the denial of access socially, politically and historically difficult in Scandinavia (Naturvårdsverket 2011). This is not to say that land ownership and a "nobility" did not develop in Scandinavia; they did, but they did so with distinctions from the rest of Europe, and even within Scandinavia there are differences which have historic origins. Regardless of the genesis, the everyman's right has remained in place; indeed in Sweden it is mentioned in the Constitution, though not enshrined in law. Aspects of the concept have been modified and clarified by law in Sweden. This codification defines what is not allowed, but does not really describe the scope of access (Naturvårdsverket 2011). As Bengtsson (2004) writes, in Sweden the list of what is acceptable is composed of low-impact activities, while high-impact extractive activities, such as timber harvesting and hunting, are not only well regulated but for private lands they are protected as property rights. The idea of everyman's right forms the basis for a culture of stewardship. It defines a framework for community access to public forest lands, and indeed to the landscape as a whole.

Both countries share a tradition of access, but despite many affiliations there are profound social and political differences. These are in no small part the product of history. Finland's economy, political system and institutions are the complex product of its proximity to present-day Russia, and of course the former Soviet Union, its late independence from Imperial Russia (something gained only at the end of the Russian revolution), and war. Finland also suffered a post-independence civil war which divided the country along class lines. Swedish history over the past century is not nearly as discordant. Even the granting of independence to Norway was a mundane affair when compared with Finnish history in the decades preceding the Second World War.

Finland was part of Sweden and then Russia, but Swedish is still spoken in parts of Finland. There is even a Swedish-language forest owners' association in Finland, the Svenska lantbruksproducenternas centralförbund. The countries maintain connections through history and language, investment and corporate ownership. The latter aspect has seen Finnish companies gain a significant share of Sweden's forest industry, demonstrating the global significance and versatility of Finland's forest products companies. Regardless of the many changes that each country has experienced, concepts of access and a strong forest identity remain socially ingrained. But access does not guarantee the right to a say in how forests are managed.

North American community forestry approaches are overwhelmingly focused on rethinking the rules of access and control over public forests. The notion of access in this context tends to be a matter of defining the conventions of extraction, while in Finland and Sweden it is about softer, less intrusive uses. Changing tenure relationships would seem easy when the land is publically owned; of course in reality it is not simple. Earlier (in Chapter 7) we noted in a case study drawn from the US southwest that there can be strong institutional opposition to changing the tenure status of public lands to accommodate community forestry. Instead, communities settle for improving the communicative context and "reforming" and broadening access to the resource. The North American relationship with forest tenure seems angst-ridden. Canadians are often rethinking forest tenure, but never enact significant change, and the institutional and legal context in the United States makes radical tenure change unlikely if not politically and socially intractable. And in a case of the "grass is always greener," some like to look to other jurisdictions for answers to their resource management problems.

The cover of the December 2007 edition of the *Report on Business*[1] features a conifer sapling, a glossy black background and the title "This tree could save Canada: What we can learn from the new kind of forest." The inside article extols the efficiency and innovation of the Finnish forest industry, Finnish forest policy and indirectly the benefits of private forest ownership – the latter being a key economic and social characteristic of the Finnish forest landscape (see Figure 8.2). Many of the arguments favorably made about the state of the Finnish forest industry could also be applied to Sweden. The envious treatment apparent in the commentary is not uncommon. There is

Figure 8.2 Logging in central Sweden. Education and training are important aspects of the forest sector and the forest management strategies of both Sweden and Finland. The belief is that a skilled workforce supports efficient and better harvesting techniques, and may make the implementation of environmental regulations easier at the stand level. Forestry is arguably the most stable part of forest sector employment (photo: K. Hanna).

an episodic habit in Canada (seemingly less so in the United States) of looking to Scandinavia as a potential model for forest policy.

The success of the Finnish and Swedish forest industries no doubt has a great deal to do with investments in product innovation, education and training that can be much higher than Canada's, and a forest policy setting forest land that has emphasized fiber production through intensive forestry (Hanna 2010). It may also have a good deal to do with the social importance that forests and forest communities have in each nation. The forest industries are not only significant contributors to the Swedish and Finnish economies; forest-derived livelihoods anchor strong regional identities within each nation, and indeed help to define the global image of each nation as places dominated by pristine forests, clean water and large tracts of wilderness. The reality can be a bit disappointing. While there is no doubting the beauty of either country, their forests have largely become fiber farms, well managed to be sure, but often devoid of the diversity, randomness and apparent wildness that less intensively managed forests often possess. This long decline in environmental quality has in recent decades become a source of policy conflict.

Neither Finland nor Sweden features a community forestry movement, or institutional structures that are like the community forestry movement or the community forest tenures we can see in North America. Yet the notion of community connections to forests, and emergent conflicts over forest use, are strong themes in both nations; and community values, often personified in private owner-ship, have greatly shaped forest policy, turning forests into what might be termed "political space" (St Martin 2001; Swyngedouw 2005; Pinkerton *et al.* 2008). This is a quality forests have assumed because of new debates over their role as a fiber source serving the neoliberal setting. But, as we noted above, there is also an age-old tradition of access to forests, mostly regardless of ownership, which is quite different from anything still present in North America. This tradition shapes the image of forests as something more than political space but expands the definition of forested lands as "socio-cultural spaces" with values and expectations of use that are historically embedded in contemporary culture and politics. This highlights a need to consider community forestry as a more complex idea than the simple assignment of tenure, or community forestry as a conflict response. We have emphasized these points in the previous chapters of this book, and we are not changing course. Rather we see that in an institutional context composed largely of individually and industrially owned forests, the idea of community forestry may have less to do with ownership than it does with ideas of access, participation in decision-making, political accountability and age-old concepts of the right of access. What has emerged is community forestry achieved through a culture of stewardship and collaboration, rather than full control through collective ownership. As for conflict, it seems to remain a constant feature in the community forest dis-course, and despite the halcyon image that the *Report on Business* painted of Finland's forest sector, as we noted above neither Finland's nor Sweden's forest sector is immune from conflict or the policy changes it tends to prompt. The policy evolution in both countries has come about in no small part as a response in part to national and regional arguments about how forests should be used and managed. The "new kind of forest" lauded in the *Report on Business* is really a fiber farm, and increasingly many Finns and Swedes find that to be far from appealing.

OWNERSHIP

The tenure of forest land in Finland and Sweden is quite distinctive when compared with North America. The great majority of productive forest land in both the United States and Canada is publically held while in the two Scandinavian countries private ownership is the principal form. But there are also differences between Sweden and Finland. The land area of Sweden is about 41 million hectares, and about 27 million hectares is forested (67% of the total land area), while 23 million hectares of this is productive forest land (METLA 2009; Sveaskog 2011). In Sweden, individuals own about 50% of forested lands. The remainder is owned by private companies (26%), state companies (about 15% is owned by Sveaskog, a state-owned forest company), "other private owners" (6%, about half of which is in the Swedish Forest commons), other state organizations (3%), and other public owners (1%) (Skogsstyrelsen 2010: 25).[2] In 2009 there were 330,802 forest owners. The number of forest entities (owned by single owners) is about 228,000, of which 66% are locally owned. Swedish forest owners' associations have about 111,000 members accounting for an area of approximately 6.2 million hectares (Skogsstyrelsen 2010).

In Finland the profile of ownership also sees private holdings accounting for most forested lands. It is with respect to state ownership that Finland differs most notably from Sweden.[3] Forested lands cover about 22 million hectares of Finland (72% of the total land area), of which some 20 million hectares are available for harvesting. About 82% of the growing stock is softwood. Individuals own about 52% of forested land, while private companies own almost 8%. The profile of individual ownership shows that farmers and pensioners own about two-thirds (one-third each) of such lands; 50% of individual owners in Finland actually live on their holdings, and another 17% live in the same municipality. The profile of local ownership is essentially the same as in Sweden. There has been a marked increase in the number of pensioners who own forest land, and the number of people who no longer live on their holdings has also increased. In contrast to the North American setting, local and federal governments own about 5%, and management of these forests is not without controversy (Hanna *et al.* 2011).

Regarding tenure, the most notable differences between the two nations are both the scale of state ownership and the institutional arrangements for management of these lands. In Finland the national government owns some 35% of forest land. This is markedly higher than in Sweden (about twice the percentage of productive forest land), and unlike Sweden, the Finnish state retains direct control over these lands. Finish state forests (about 9 million hectares) are directly managed by Metsähallitus (Finnish forest and park agency) making it the largest owner of forests in Europe. In Sweden, state-owned forest lands are "held" by Sveaskog, a forest company wholly owned by the Swedish state. The Skogsstyrelsen (Swedish forest agency) oversees compliance with regulation and forest law(s), but does not directly manage state lands or deal with the sale of timber. Most state-owned forest land in Finland is located in the northern regions of the country, and in recent years there have been increasing conflicts over the impacts of harvesting on reindeer management. In Sweden the majority of Sveaskog's lands are located in Norrbotten and Västerbotten, in the Bergslag area, and in central Götaland (Sveaskog 2011) – areas mostly concentrated in the north, a distribution somewhat similar to Finland's.

Starting in the 1990s, Sweden began to change the ownership arrangements of state forests. At first about 4.3 million hectares were transferred to Sveaskog, but large tracts of low productivity (that is to say, little industrial value) were transferred to the National Property Board, a good portion of it being mountain wilderness (Nylund 2010: 16). Sveaskog retained some 3.2 million is productive forest land or 14% of *productive* forest land, which makes Sveaskog the largest single forest owner in the country and the fourth largest forest owner in Europe (Nylund 2010; Sveaskog 2011). Originally Sveaskog included some processing operations, but these have been sold. While Sveaskog manages what are public lands it also sells land to private owners, and as Nylund (2010: 17) notes, the corporatist model that Sweden has adopted for state forest lands now means that establishing forest reserves requires that land be purchased at market value from Sveaskog, rather than simply transferring control (ownership) from one agency to another – the model when the State Forest Service managed such areas.

Forest sector employment in both nations has shown a similar trend in recent decades. While it appears relatively stable overall, in recent years there have been moderate declines. For example, in 1998,[4] the forest sector (which includes both forestry and the forest industries) in Finland employed about 96,000 people (about 4.1% of national employment), but by 2006 this had dropped to 90,000 and just two years later in 2008 it was 82,000 (about 3.2% of national employment). The steepest decline has been in the forest industries (processing and wood products). In 1998 about 72,000 people worked in this half of the sector, but by 2008 the number had declined to 58,000. In the pulp and paper industries alone some 41,000 people were employed, and by 2008 the number was just 27,000. However, if we look at forestry (harvesting and silvicultural activities) the number employed in 1998 was 24,000, and in 2008 it was still 24,000. In the intervening years there were variations in forestry employment numbers, but rarely a shift of more than 1,000 jobs.

In Sweden we can see a similar pattern. In 1995 total employment in the forest sector was about 120,000, but by 2009 the number was 97,000.[5] In the forest industries the drop for the same period was from 92,000 employed to 69,000. As in Finland the largest number of jobs lost was in the pulp and paper industries: a decline from 48,000 in 1995 to 33,000 by 2009. Just as we see in Finland, Swedish forestry employment in 2009 was about 25,000, the same as it was over a decade ago. However, just as in Finland there were job losses in forestry in some of the intervening years, and sometimes the change was substantial – the year 2003 saw forestry jobs in Sweden drop to 16,000. In both countries after an initial period of advances in the mechanization of harvesting (which mostly pre-dates the years quoted here), the employment declines in forestry slowed. Subsequent variations in forestry employment reflect timber demand and regional availability. The reasons for processing employment decline are complex. These relate to changes in product mix, corporate concentration, mechanization and other rationalization processes. However, production and wood consumption in both nations has increased. A review of wood consumption by the forest industries shows a steady increase from 1998 to 2008 (METLA 2001, 2009, 2010; Skogsstyrelsen 2010). In other words, more wood is being processed with fewer workers than in previous decades, but it still takes roughly the same number of people to fell and transport wood for processing.

A great challenge for both nations will be the changing nature of demand for domestic wood. It is argued that the sector is far from stable and is indeed entering a period of flux that will likely reshape not only management, but also the respective roles of key economic, policy and societal actors (Donner-Amnell, 2011). With increasing competition from other locales in the paper and building products sectors, including Canada, the role of these traditional industries and their demand for wood will decline. What will replace them is speculative. Donner-Amnell (2011) suggests that bio-energy and chemical production will play an important role. If this comes to be, then interesting questions emerge about how such a new industrial setting might shape forest management and the role that landowners will play in defining the future forest industry. The reality is that forest owners will likely have little say in the shape of a new forest industry. Change will

Figure 8.3 "Working for forest owners." Forest owner organizations in Finland and Sweden provide a strong voice when dealing with government, and serve to counter-balance the power and influence of industry and environmental lobbyists. In addition to advocacy for the forest-owning community, these organizations also help with forest planning, selling timber and managing logging or other forestry activities. There are few North American equivalents (photo: K. Hanna).

be determined by larger market forces, most of which are beyond Finland's border. What landowners may be able to greatly affect are the policies that determine forest management.

Each nation has many strong landowner associations (Figure 8.3). These have variable forms, and provide benefits which can include wood brokerage, managing timber sales and logging, tax and estate planning, silvicultural advice and planning, and advocacy (Kittredge 2003). These organizations provide a collective approach to dealing with government and regulation. They have emerged as powerful voices, and in Finland they have no doubt played an important part in shaping policy aimed at private lands. Forest owner organizations also provide an important counter-balance to the power and influence of industry and corporate lobbyists, and of environmental organizations. It is difficult to find a North American equivalent with either the benefit level or the political strength that is found amongst forest owner associations in Sweden and Finland.

In North America there is a political–economic compact between government, industry and labor, certainly in Canada and with some regional variations in the United States. This compact has not proven to be resilient to environmental conflict. Labor seems the loser, in part because industrial innovation has reduced the number of workers required to produce wood products, and because industry and government have sought compromise with environmental groups in order to address conflict and to retain markets. In contrast, the Scandinavian compact is between industry, government and landowners (J. Donner-Amnell, personal communication, October 2011). It is a relationship that has proven resistant to environmental demands and is perhaps a testament to the political–social power of small-scale forest ownership. Such ownership, with many individuals, while not wholly immune to environmental pressures, does provide a strong political foundation for blunting their impacts and delaying the implementation of change.

THE EVOLUTION OF SWEDISH POLICY: FROM DICTATES TO PERSUASIVE PLANNING

Swedish forest policy from the late 1970s to the early 2000s certainly emphasized fiber production in part to reduce the import of wood for its industry. Implementation of the broad objective was realized mostly through the Skogvårdsstreleyse (county forest boards) and the national Skogsstyrelsen. Nylund (2010: 16) writes that 1979 to 1992 marks the summit of the boards' works with strong requirements for management plans and compulsory management recommendations for owners and subsidies for industry operations. This culture of intervention and compulsory planning, while seeking to "improve" forest management for the purpose of fiber production, also saw little room for including conservation or preservation values. It was in many respects symbolic of the welfare state politics that affected all aspects of Swedish life.

Changes in government, which saw Sweden gradually move away from the ubiquitous role of government, also led to changes in Swedish forest policy. Most notable, perhaps, was the creation of Sveaskog, and the private sector (neoliberal) model of forest management and ownership it represents; an approach embodied in privatization and corporate control, albeit one owned by the state. In 1993 the compulsory requirement for "individual forest plans" was repealed (Nylund 2010). The most intrusive aspect of forest planning imposed on individual landowners changed with the introduction of less onerous planning approaches ultimately allowing landowners to make decisions that reflected individual values. Landowners were no longer required to manage for timber production.

Swedish forest management was hardly devoid of conflict. During the 1970s, Swedish environmental protection and forestry agencies were essentially "missing-in-action" when it came to forestry operations (Frisén 2001; Nylund 2010). The logging of high elevation areas and programs to convert natural forests into plantation forests were particularly controversial. Industrial logging practices in the north have had major impacts on reindeer habitat, with declines in some regions of up to 50% of historic winter grazing grounds (Berg *et al.* 2008). In 1975 the *Forestry Act* was revised to require forest owners to pay heed to nature and cultural conservation interests. But subsidies and contradictory requirements and subsidies remained in place: notably, the requirement to cut over-aged stock; a requirement to restock unproductive lands (which might include old grazing lands, mixed forests or other biotopes); and subsidies for replanting agricultural land, draining wetlands and fertilizing bogs, and constructing logging roads and new roads in roadless areas (Frisén 2001; Nylund, 2010). The shift to a policy context that increasingly emphasizes environmental protection came after several decades that saw Swedish forest management broadly criticized within Europe. Subsidies were also provided to convert "natural" forests in northern Sweden, which were euphemistically and perhaps strategically labeled skrapskogar (garbage forests), into plantation forests. Environmental organizations in Sweden and Europe threatened boycotts of Swedish wood products, and this was to lead to a rethinking of the policy tools being used, though it would hardly bring about a rejection of the core fiber production objective (Bäckström 2001; Nylund 2010).

In the early 1990s, environmental policy in Sweden began to change. In addition to broad initiatives to conserve biodiversity, there was a new (some might say renewed) emphasis on expanding areas of preservation. With respect to forest management, the specific policies moved beyond an accent on aesthetics to gradually include "biodiversity action plans," and eventually national environmental objectives, one of which was the "Living Forests" initiative. These changes came about in no small part because of growing opposition within Sweden to forest policy that was degrading the natural qualities of the nation's remaining natural areas. The Swedish paradox is that the process of reform aimed at reducing state intervention in forest management and processing, arguably a neoliberal economic and land-use reform response, was also accompanied by a rising consciousness about the loss of environmental quality – an awareness reflected somewhat in new policies and laws. Further change seems increasingly likely, given the shifting public demands.

Swedish land-use policies can contain interesting contradictions which likely reflect conflicted thinking about how best to move away from the welfare state model. Forest policy has been reformed. It is less intrusive for landowners, but it struggles to balance environmental protection with fiber production. In some respects this reflects the social and ideological diversity that has become more pronounced in recent Swedish political life. Nylund (2010) chronicles a shift within the Swedish political landscape that illustrates the changing nature of policy. From the 1950s to the 1990s the center-left political parties favored industrial development and fiber production – policies that would become the basis for environmental protest – whilst the non-socialist parties promoted rural policies. Now there are new alliances and a bit of an about-face. The Social Democrats, Greens and leftist parties champion a relatively "radical" environmental message, while center-right parties back policies that support both rural and industrial forest development (Nylund 2010).

The policy setting has moved to focus on guiding individual landowners in order to achieve broader economic and social, and now environmental, goals. We noted above that a community forest system akin to the models seen in Canada and the United States does not really exist. One tenure form in Sweden would appear to come close, but there are important distinctions. The Swedish Forest Commons are a form of tenure that few outside Sweden are likely to be familiar with. Commons have been well discussed in terms of the rules of membership, institutional context and the rules of collective action and decision-making (e.g. Kiser and Ostrom 1982; Ostrom 1990; Arnold 1993) and the evolution of the concept (e.g. Burger and Gochfield 1998); the Forest Commons were institutionally defined in the late nineteenth century, and the intent was to provide a foundation for regional development (Carlsson 2001). While the state supports their existence, the regulatory context is complex and it has evolved since the commons were formalized. Carlsson (2001) comments that increasingly some of the rules created by the Swedish state actually serve to erode the commons by imposing conditions of ownership, transfer and governance that are incompatible with the foundations of the commons.

Initially the commons were apportioned on a shareholder basis, but no one could be a shareholder without owning a forest or farm (Carlsson 2001). Today the ownership pattern is complex, and the conditions describe what is more a form of collective ownership rather than a true commons. Forest companies also hold shares in some of the commons adding to the complication of ownership. Forest Commons have a legal foundation and are governed for the benefit of their members. While they are run according to the wishes of members, the governance model is based on membership, but they can be at variance with the liberal democratic context that surrounds them. This occasionally causes conflict when the values and objectives of a commons differ from those of surrounding communities or the changing regulatory setting created by the state.

Certification represents another approach to forest governance, and provides an additional set of principles to those provided by government (Schlüter *et al.* 2009, as quoted in Nylund 2010). Both the Swedes and the Finns have taken quite well to the concept, but differently. About half of productive forest land in Sweden is certified and one label, the Forest Stewardship Council (FSC), alone accounts most of this (Boström 2003; Nylund 2010). Certification has its origins with environmental groups who pushed the concept as a way of influencing production methods by shaping consumer preferences. Swedish environmental organizations working with other European groups pressured retailers to demand verification of the sustainable management of forests from which wood for Swedish products was taken (Boström 2003; Hysing 2009). It is an alternative form of regulation, self-directed and initially voluntary. As more companies have embraced certification in Sweden it has lost its potential as a "marketing advantage" tool and has become the norm in forest production standards. It is a tool for enhancing corporate standing, and it is a marketing tool, but in reality it does little to enhance competitiveness (Boström 2002; Nylund 2010).

In the Swedish context, FSC certification has proven unwieldy for owners of small forest holdings, and neither the Forest Owners Association nor Greenpeace has joined the FSC system (Nylund 2010). Instead, owners themselves, along with other European forest owner associations, have endorsed a separate process. This was originally called the Pan European Forest Certification Scheme (PEFC), and since it is now used beyond Europe it has been rebranded the Programme for the Endorsement of Forest Certification (Hysing 2009; Nylund 2010). No environmental organization has joined the PEFC in Sweden (Hysing 2009). Both systems have aspects that recognize regional needs. The PEFC incorporates regional differences into its standards to recognize the differences between northern and southern forests and between their management characteristics. The Sámi people participated in the national standard setting and had their customary herding rights included in national standards.

Certification was initially viewed by environmental organizations as an alternative way of achieving better management than government was willing to encourage or require, and for communities it initially seemed a "better way" to incorporate community values into forestry practice. It was to be a form of governance without government (Hysing 2009). In what might be a case of too much success, a myriad of certification schemes have been developed, not only for wood, but the model has been disseminated to other resource sectors. But their efficacy and integrity are increasingly questioned, and the capacity of certification to effectively integrate community concerns into forest management is far from assured. Environmental organizations face a challenge; if they choose to withdraw support from certification organizations they may lose their influence over standards and enforcement (Nylund 2010). As well, far from achieving "governing without government," certification in the Swedish case includes government involvement. Both Sveaskog and the National Property Board have certified their holdings, and the government has helped to facilitate FSC negotiations, has provided mediation services and was consulted on various issues (Hysing 2009). The larger policy setting has also been aligned, and reformed with certification in mind, and while the relationship is not explicit, it is certainly implicit. Certification was seen as a way of achieving a modicum of deregulation and the transfer of responsibilities for management standards from a regulatory context to a non-government governance setting, but government has retained an important role by helping to shape the context that supports certification.

The Swedish policy setting has taken on the characteristics of "roll-back" neoliberalism where state organizations, law and regulation and the objectives of public policy increasingly seek to promote privatization (Lockie and Higgins 2007; Pinkerton *et al.* 2008). But elements of roll-out neoliberalism also exist. We see in recent Swedish policy – in forest management, environmental protection and protected areas designation – an emphasis on technocratic management, which is evident in certification standards and approval processes, coupled with what bears the characteristics of a profoundly interventionist social and environmental protection agenda (Lockie and Higgins 2007; Pinkerton *et al.* 2008). McCarthy (2005, 2006) characterizes the community forestry setting in the United States as a hybrid between rising neoliberalism and simultaneous trends in the protection and management of protected areas and public forest lands. The Swedish experience and evolution of forest policy can be explained in the same way. There has been a gradual transformation from intrusive policies and a strong regulatory setting focused solely on fiber production, to a less coercive regulatory regime and an emphasis on governance through certification as a surrogate form of state regulation. The importance of fiber production remains, but a place for environmental protection has been created. The Swedish Forest Commons, long established by state direction, are also now being fundamentally reshaped by the implementation of neoliberal policies. The government also remains involved in certification – as a not-so-well-disguised hand gently promoting and guiding the establishment and implementation of the certification process and the promotion of its wider application.

FINNISH POLICY AND PLANNING: THE HIERARCHICAL DISINTEGRATION OF PARTICIPATION

The Finnish experience from the 1970s onward saw an emphasis on fiber production, as in Sweden, though the policies were not coercive. While the Finnish approach has tended to stress support for woodlot management and soft instruments, such as tax and subsidy policies, and may appear to be less coercive than the Swedish approach, Finnish law also dictates fundamental forest management techniques. As in Sweden, even-aged management is required and clear-felling (clearcutting) is the order of the day. Policies in the past have also supported expansion of wood-producing lands, such as the draining of wetlands to grow wood. In recent decades, conflict has emerged over forest management, and some intensive forest management policies have been have been criticized and rethought (Hellström 2001; Pykälä 2007; Raitio 2008). The requirement for even-aged management is being rethought, and the Forest Law will likely soon be changed to allow for uneven-aged forestry. Such shifts are in no small part a reflection of social change and different community values, and they seem late when compared with Canadian and US experience with such silvicultural systems. Increasingly it seems that Finns desire a different kind of forest, one with more diversity and complexity, and forest that will yield the aesthetic and recreational qualities that an affluent and more urbanized population wants. In Finland such reforms are still resisted by some in industry and even in professional forestry. Nor is uneven-aged management a panacea; it may not yield all the qualities that

Figure 8.4 Birch forest at Kolin kansallispuisto (Koli National Park) in eastern Finland. By North American standards this is a small park. It is well visited and contains small remnants of relatively untouched forest. The surrounding area is dominated by private woodlots, and the forest industry has a major presence in the region. Parklands are woven into a landscape that is largely private and very well used (photo: K. Hanna).

proponents envision. Achieving something akin to a "natural" forest demands a more complex management response: it means mixing silvicultural systems, increasing permanent preservation areas, considering shifting preservation (where preservation areas are temporal depending on the ecological characteristics) and objectives, and making tough decisions about uses – in other words, a much stronger planning response.

In the late 1990s, the European Union made it a responsibility for member nations to prepare national forestry programs. Forest owner associations have a powerful voice in Finnish forest policy, as do forest product companies. Finnish forestry is very much oriented toward creating a setting that provides the basis for industrial competitiveness and a reliable wood fiber supply. These fundamental objectives are evident in a hierarchical policy process that has evolved to strengthen the timber-oriented management of private lands and through education, skills development and taxation to create conditions that support what may well be the world's most technologically advanced and vertically integrated forest industry (see Figure 8.4).

The Finnish forest policy setting is an interesting blend of non-obligatory policies, statute-based regulations and variable transparency requirements. The policy and planning framework has four levels. At the top is the National Forest Program (NFP) which was developed as a national, wide-ranging set of forest management objectives, but which lacks a regulatory means of enforcement (Hanna *et al.* 2011). It is a statement of objectives (with guidelines for achievement) but it also has a strategic quality. The NFP does, however, affect the allocation of public funds to programs and activities, and as such it has a persuasive quality that helps shape environmental and social considerations (Hanna *et al.* 2011). The NFP is the pinnacle of a model that eventually has its greatest operational impact at the level of individual landowners and state forest managers, where macro-policy seems to be interpreted, but not really commanded.

At the regional level, forest authorities prepare Regional Forest Programs. The Regional Programs really have an information and guidance role without being binding for decision-makers (Kokko 2009; Hanna *et al.* 2011). This guideline nature essentially makes them "a suggestion for good behavior," which might be a tad cynical since they do seem to be followed, but they also lack a certain force. Preparation of a Regional Program does include some public partici-pation, but the impact is debated (Hanna *et al.* 2011). Some (e.g. Tikkanen 2006) hold that participation in the regional process has not been effective in seeing environmental values incorporated into operational and practice outcomes. Others suggest that the impact of participation is realized through processes of knowledge building and social learning, rather than binding prescriptions. Leskinen (2004), for example, writes that participation in developing Regional Forest Programs has influenced outcomes (practice and operational) through a soft route that gives emphasis to improved learning, rela-tionship building, knowledge sharing and better overall interest representation.

At the next level we have the Regional Forest Plans (not to be confused with Regional Forest Programs). Regional Forest Plans are more localized than a Regional Program, and it is at this level that the operational perspective emerges. This level is seen as a crucial part of implementing the broad policy objectives of the NFP and implementing them at the local level (Tikkanen and Kurttila 2007). But it is also at this level that public participation essentially ends. Regional Plans are not usually made available for public review, the contextual information they contain is not often available, and even if they are provided as a response to a request, there is really no mechanism for participation or consultation (Hanna *et al.* 2011).

A Regional Forest Plan supports the last level of planning, called Holding-specific Forest Plans. These have a 10-year horizon, and they apply to specific forest properties not owned by the Finnish state – those owned by individuals, local governments, parishes and industry (Hanna *et al.* 2011). Stand-level (property-level) planning is intended to lead forest owners in making choices about forest use rather than necessarily dictate actions. Holding-specific Forest Plans have a proprietary quality, and forest authorities will not make the plan available for review without the permission of the landowner (Tapion taskukirja 2002, as quoted in Hanna *et al.* 2011). When harvesting activities are about to occur, land owners prepare a Forest Use Declaration, which is an "announcement of intention," given to authorities before forestry (harvesting or other silvicultural) activities begin. While Declarations are ostensibly a public document, they are neither published nor circulated to neighbors or other stakeholders. As Pölönen (personal communication, June 2010) comments, it creates a setting where the community has to know what is going on by seeing it happen, instead of finding out through the authorities, since they do not often advertise such operations. In a context where an announcement is not really an announcement, the notion of the "public availability" of a Declaration rings a bit hollow.

Participation at the level of the National Forest Program focuses on broad policy development, rather than being incorporated into ongoing, site-level implementation. Participation disintegrates as the planning and policy implementation process moves from the development of national policy, to region and site-specific plans. The expectation is that since participation is included in the development of the NFP it will be reflected in planning at the local level. While that may happen, a key challenge in implementation is overcoming the assumption that an idea once conceived at the macro-level will be faithfully put into effect at the community level.

As the manager of state forests, the agency Metsähallitus has a contradictory mandate (Raitio 2008; Hanna *et al.* 2011). On the one hand Metsähallitus is required to generate revenue for the government though the sale of timber and other natural resources, but on the other it is also supposed to support and integrate a number of socio-environmental goals into forest management – for example conservation of biodiversity conservation, forest-based employment, recreation opportunities, reindeer herding and the activities that support the indigenous Sámi culture (Raitio 2008; Hanna *et al.* 2011). However, since it operates like a business enterprise, Metsähallitus has a fiscal stake in its plans and is seen by many critics as being biased toward timber production (Raitio 2008).

Starting in the early 1990s, criticism of Metsähallitus' approach to forest management began to grow. This reproach focused on the agency's perceived lack of concern for non-timber values. In response, the agency has gradually added collaborative approaches and new opportunities for public participation in its planning processes. Metsähallitus' landscape-level responses included broad changes to forest management and harvesting, and more protected areas (Raitio 2008). The agency also established stakeholder working groups to advise planning processes, and public input is solicited through meetings and interactive websites (Hanna *et al.* 2011). Though consultation occurs, its impacts on forest management are disputed. Some see the process of evaluation of different management options that occurs in planning as really being focused on timber production and forestry-dependent employment, while impacts on biodiversity protection, recreation values and non-timber livelihoods are neglected or considered only half-heartedly (Hanna *et al.* 2011). This is perhaps most evident when it comes to considering the impacts of forestry activities on the livelihoods of the indigenous Sámi people (Raitio 2008). The extent and nature of forestry impacts on reindeer herding is one of the most contested issues for forestry planning in northern Finland. Forestry actions cover vast areas of Sámi traditional territory and natural resource planning processes have not really developed credibility with those most affected (Raitio 2008).

Metsähallitus and the forest industry have been criticized by domestic and foreign environmental organizations for their approaches to forestry. The involvement of German organizations has been contentious, and referred to by supporters of the forest industry as the "second German assault" – an allusion to the wholesale destruction German troops caused in northern Finland on their retreat into Norway during the Second World War. As Raitio (2008) relates, divisions and lingering conflict are omnipresent and reflect the different perspectives on preservation, traditional livelihoods and industrial forestry that permeate the forest management discourse in northern Finland to this day. There is little sign that they will be resolved to everyone's liking (Raitio 2008). Regardless, conflict has affected policy change.

Nylund (2010: 22) characterizes the Finnish approach to developing the NFP as including "wide stakeholder participation" and ultimately having a stronger status than that the Swedish equivalent. But conflict exists in Finnish forest management (Hellström 2001). Others, however, are less sanguine about the resulting Finnish NFP, if not necessarily about the process of putting it together – pointing out that consultation and participation were indeed part of developing the Program. However, many multiple-use and conflict issues were left unsettled, and there are no mechanisms for solving disputes about conflicting land uses (Primmer and Kyllönen 2006; Kokko 2009; Hanna et al. 2011). The participatory influence in the Finnish context seems inconsistent, and there can be little doubt that although the NFP includes attention to environmental quality, it is very much about providing timber. In this respect, Finland's policy and planning objectives may be no different than other important timber-producing jurisdictions.

In terms of the paradigmatic approach, Finnish forest policy is distinctive from the Swedish model. There have been advances in expanding protected areas largely in northern Finland, but forestry activities on private lands are typically not subject to review or assessment, even in those cases where they would undeniably cause significant negative environmental or social impacts (Pölönen 2007; Pykälä 2007). The approach has been to develop and improve inventories while hoping that such information collection and provision would have an impact on operational activities. The results are certainly mixed. Participation has improved as the NFP has been developed and implemented, but the impact and indeed requirements for broader public participation in forest planning and management disintegrate as the process moves from macro-national and regional programs (which are suggestive, hopeful and broad objectives-oriented) to the level of site or property-specific decision-making.

About 95% of Finland's commercial forests are certified under the PEFC system (Keskitalo 2009). Membership is composed of industry and forest owner groups. No environmental organizations belong to the PEFC in Finland, but Metsähallitus does. The preference for the PEFC system stems in part from early mistrust of the FSC process led by environmental organizations, and instead industry and landowner groups developed the PEFC (Keskitalo 2009). Certification lacks transparency in communicating the results of audits and surveillance (Pappila 2011). On the other hand, Pappila does comment that certification has likely enhanced learning amongst forest owners, and can form the foundation of a broader discussion about forest management. It remains to be seen whether such a discourse will generate the capacity to affect much change in forest management or foster openness in the planning process. Certification has not notably changed forest management. The PEFC includes no requirement for the consideration of social or community objectives; it contains no provisions for taking into account the impact of forestry activities on hunting and game habitat, berry or mushroom picking, or other common Finnish forest activities (Keskitalo 2009; Pappila 2011). Certification in the Finnish context is really a marketing tool.

BUILDING A CULTURE OF STEWARDSHIP

The absence or presence of revolution, occupation war and civil war has shaped civil society in each nation. The resulting "cultures" of individualism and willingness to accept state intervention in private forest management are quite different, though they follow similar patterns of broad public interests, notably the shift from a public–industry–government compact that wholly supported fiber production, to a setting where other land-use values are emergent, increasingly vocal and progressively more influential. The individualism that characterizes Finnish society also makes politically difficult the development of forest policy that would be seen as too intrusive on the property rights of individuals (Hanna *et al.* 2011). Social acceptance would be largely absent for a regulatory approach that does anything to seriously weaken landowner's rights, or open planning and decision-making for private forests to public review and approval. Thus, while Swedish forest policy for private lands has in the past been imposed, Finnish forest policy for private forests might be seen as being more advisory in tone, and the adoption and implementation of initiatives that affect private lands tend to be the products of governance processes that are politically wary of intruding too much on the "rights" of landowners. As the Finnish and Swedish economies shift, the forest industry may account for a smaller portion of national employment and a smaller part of the export economy, and the policy setting will also change. This is a trend affecting many major forest-products producing nations. Raitio's (2008) work in northern Finland highlights the role of a growing environmental movement in Finland. which, though focused on the management of state forests, is also gradually turning its attention to private land use. This concern centers on the impacts of harvesting activities on biodiversity and other elements of environmental quality, but it also includes a growing social and community discussion about integrating non-timber values into planning for private forest lands. But managing for timber production also reflects the values of a significant portion of Finnish and Swedish societies.

As populations have grown and countrysides have changed, the regulatory setting has struggled to balance a better explanation of *jokamiehenoikeus* or *allemansrätten* with the social and cultural values and the community and individual expectations that have long defined the idea. The concept is a cultural force, but it is not a participation process, at least directly. The idea that access is a cherished right is likely reflected in the high rates of participation among Swedes and Finns in forest-based activities, and it helps to keep the very real impacts of forest management and resulting landscape change in the public eye. Several years ago, on a tour of private woodlots in Sweden, an American forester asked how much interest the locals had in logging on private woodlots. A Swedish colleague replied that with respect to both private and public forestry, "it's hard to hide much when you have a good portion of the population roaming across the countryside at any given time of year."[6] The same can be said for Finland.

Whereas community forestry movements have emerged in North America as part of a social response to waning economic fortunes and forest decline, a similar problem foundation in Scandinavia has also produced a demand for more community control, only one manifest not in terms of tenure but in terms of access to the policy process. The response in Sweden and Finland has not focused on changing the structure of tenure; there is no serious social or political interest in doing that, nor is it necessary, but there is great interest in changing the policy process and the rules of management. There are differences between the two Scandinavian countries, but what has emerged is an emphasis on opening up decision-making and building new governance tools that seek to improve participation. But, as we have noted, the efficacy of these efforts is much debated.

The sense of community involvement in forest management is defined through ownership and participation in organizations that advances owner objectives. Participation helps, but there seems little interest in creating the type of community forest structures that have emerged in Canada, and to a lesser extent the United States. Instead access and use are culturally, historically and socially defined. The "community forest" surrounds communities, regardless of land ownership. The tradition of access supports a community understanding of the state of forests and a timely knowledge of changes to forested landscapes; as well, it has created an acceptance of uses that are both intensive and temperate. It is also that right to access the land that has led to public demands for policy change and different approaches to forestry, irrespective of ownership. A tradition and culture of community access has created an ethos of awareness and a strong social interest in how forests are managed, regardless of ownership. This may well constitute a different form of community forestry.

NOTES

1 A magazine published by the *Toronto Globe and Mail*, the article was authored by Konrad Yakabuski.
2 Percentages are approximate; methods and reporting do vary from year to year, so absolute comparisons are not always possible, though trends may be estimated.
3 Finnish forest data is quoted from METLA (2009).
4 In our comparison 1998 is used as the base year for Finland and 1995 for Sweden. The differences reflect the different formats of the forestry statistical yearbooks by each nation. Employment data here is quoted from METLA (2001) and METLA (2009).
5 Swedish employment data is quoted from Skogsstyrelsen (2010).
6 A comment noted by K. Hanna during a forestry tour near Östersund.

REFERENCES

Arnold, J. (1993). Management of forests resources as common property. *Commonwealth Forestry Review* **72**(93): 157–61.
Bäckström, P.-O. (2001). Några erfarenheter av svensk skogspolitik. In Ekelund, H. and Hamilton, G. (eds.), *Skogspolitisk historia. Rapport 8a.* Jönköping: Skogsstyrelsen,
Bengtsson, B. (2004). *Allemansrätten – Vad säger lagen?* Stockholm: Naturvårdsverket.
Berg, A., Östlund, L. Mowen, J. and Olofsson, J. (2008). A century of logging and forestry in a reindeer herding area in northern Sweden. *Forest Ecology and Management* **256**: 1009–20.
Boström, M. (2002). *Skogen märks – Hur svensk skogscertifiering kom till och dess konsekvenser.* SCORE report. Stockholm University. Available at www.score.su. se/pdfs/2002-3.pdf.
Boström, M. (2003). How state-dependent is a non-state-driven rule-making project? The case of forest certification in Sweden. *Journal of Environmental Policy and Planning* 5(2):165–80.
Burger, J. and Gochfield, M. (1998). The tragedy of the commons 30 years later. *Environment* **40**(10): 4–27.
Carlsson, L. (2001). Keeping away from the leviathan: The case of the Swedish Forest Commons. Research paper prepared for the MOST Project on Circumpolar Coping Processes. Lulea: Lulea University of Technology.
Donner-Amnell, J. (2011). New factors challenging the character and legitimacy of forest use in Finland. Conference presentation, Yhteiskuntatieteellisen ympäristötutkimuksen seura ry Fall 2011 Colloquium. Joensuu: University of Eastern Finland.
Folke, C., Hahn, T., Olsson, P. and Norberg, J. (2005). Adaptive governance of social-ecological systems. *Annual Review of Environment and Resources* **30**: 441–73.
Frisén, R. (2001). *Skogsbruk och naturvård under ett halvt sekel, 1950–2000.* Jönköping: Skogsstyrelsen.

Hanna, K. (2010). Transition and the need for innovation in Canada's forest sector. In Mitchell, B. (ed.), *Resource and Environmental Management in Canada: Addressing Conflict and Uncertainty*. Toronto, ON: Oxford University Press.

Hanna, K., Pölönen, I. and Raitio, K. (2011). A potential role for EIA in Finnish forest planning: Learning from experiences in Ontario, Canada. *Impact Assessment and Project Appraisal*, **29**(2).

Hellström, E. (2001). *Conflict Cultures: Qualitative Comparative Analysis of Environmental Conflicts in Forestry*. Silva Fennica, Monographs 2, Helsinki: Finnish Society of Forest Science.

Hysing, E. (2009). Governing without government? The private governance of forest certification in Sweden. *Public Administration* **87**(2): 312–26.

Irvine, D. (1999). *Certification and community forestry: current trends and challenges and potential*. A background paper prepared for the World Bank/WWF Alliance on Independent Certification. Washington: World Bank/WWF Alliance on Independent Certification.

Keskitalo, E.C.H., Sandström, C., Tysiachniouk, M. and Johansson, J. (2009). Local consequences of applying international norms: Differences in the application of forest certification in northern Sweden, northern Finland, and northwest Russia. *Ecology and Society* **14**(2). Available at http://www.ecologyandsociety.org/vol14/iss2/art1/

Kiser, L. and Ostrom, E. (1982). The three worlds of action: A metatheoretical synthesis of institutional approaches. In Ostrom, E. (ed.), *Strategies of Political Inquiry*. Beverly Hills, CA: Sage.

Kittredge, D. (2003). Private forestland owners in Sweden, large-scale cooperation inaction. *Journal of Forestry* **101**(2): 41–6.

Kokko, K. (2009). A legal method and tools for evaluation the effectiveness of regulation: Safeguarding forest biodiversity in Finland. *Nordic Environmental Law Journal* **2009**: 57–78.

Lawrence, A., Anglezarke, B., Frost, B., Nolan, P. and Owen, R. (2009). What does community forestry mean in a devolved Great Britain? *International Forestry Review* **11**(2): 281–97.

Leskinen, L. (2004). Purposes and challenges of public participation in regional and local forestry in Finland. *Forest Policy and Economics* **6**: 605–18.

Lockie, S. and Higgins, V. (2007). Roll-out neoliberalism and hybrid practices of regulation in Australian Agri-Environmental Governance. *Journal of Rural Studies* **23**(1): 1–11.

McCarthy, J. (2005). Devolution in the woods: Community forestry as hybrid neoliberalism. *Environment and Planning A* **37**(6) 995–1014.

McCarthy, J. (2006). Neoliberalism and the politics of alternatives: Community forestry in British Columbia and the United States. *Annals of the Association of American Geographers* **96**(1): 84–104.

METLA (Finnish Forest Research Institute) (2001). *Forest Finland in Brief, 2001*. Joensuu: METLA.

METLA (Finnish Forest Research Institute) (2009). *Forest Finland in Brief, 2009*. Joensuu: METLA.

METLA (Finnish Forest Research Institute) (2010). *Metsätilastollinen vuosikirja (Finnish Statistical Yearbook of Forestry)*. Sastamala: Vammalan Kirjapaino Oy.

Naturvårdsverket (2011). *What is the Right of Public*. Available at http://www.naturvardsverket.se. Accessed July 14, 2011.

Nylund, J.-E. (2010). *Swedish Forest Policy since 1990 – Reforms and Consequences*. Report No. 16. Uppsala: SLU Department of Forest Products.

Ostrom, E. (1990). *Governing the Commons: The Evolution of Institutions for Collective Action*. Cambridge: Cambridge University Press.

Pappila, M. (2011). *Metsäsääntely Suomessa ja Venäjällä: Näkökulmia kestävään metsä-talouteen.* Turku: Turku University.

Pinkerton, E., Heaslip, R., Silver, J. and Furman, K. (2008). Finding "space" for comanagement of forests within the neoliberal paradigm: Rights, strategies, and tools for asserting a local agenda. *Human Ecology* 36: 343–55.

Pölönen, I. (2007). *Ympäristövaikutusten arviointimenettely. Tutkimus YVA-menettelyn oikeudellisesta asemasta ja kehittämistarpeista ympäristöllisen vaikuttavuuden näkökulmasta. [Environmental impact assessment.]* A-sarja No. 280. Jyväskylä: Suomalaisen Lakimiesyhdistyksen julkaisuja.

Primmer, E. and Kyllönen, S. (2006). Goals for public participation implied by sustainable development, and the preparatory process of the Finnish National Forest Programme. *Forest Policy and Economics* 8: 838–53.

Pykälä, J. (2007). Implementation of forest act in Finland: Does it protect the right habitats for threatened species? *Forest Ecology and Management* 242: 281–7.

Raitio, K. (2008). *"You Can't Please Everyone" – Conflict Management Practices, Frames, and Institutions in Finnish State Forests.* Publications in Social Sciences 86. Joensuu: University of Joensuu.

Schlüter, A., Stjerquist, I. and Bäckstrand, K. (2009). Not seeing the forest for the trees? The environmental effectiveness of forest certification in Sweden. *Forest Policy and Economics* 11(5–6): 375–82.

Schultz, L., Folke, C. and Olsson, P. (2007). Enhancing ecosystem management through social–ecological inventories: Lessons from Kristianstads Vatten-rike, Sweden. *Environmental Conservation* 34(2): 140–52.

Skogsstyrelsen (2010). *Skogsstatistisk årsbok 2010. [Swedish Statistical Yearbook of Forestry 2010.]* Jönköping: Skogsstyrelsen.

St Martin, K. (2001). Making space for community resource management in fisheries. *Annals of the Association of American Geographers* 91:122–42.

Sveaskog (2011). *Om Sveaskog, Skogsinnehav.* Available at http://www.sveaskog.se/Om-Sveaskog/Skogsinnehav/ Accessed July 1, 2011.

Swyngedouw, E. (2005). Governance, innovation and the citizen: The Janus face of governance-beyond-the-state. *Urban Studies* 42: 1991–2006.

Tikkanen, J. (2006). Osapuolten välinen yhteistyö yksityismetsien suunnittelussa. Metsäsuunnittelu ja ekonomia, Metsätieteellinen tiedekunta. Dissertationes Forestales 26.

Tikkanen, J. and Kurttila, M. (2007). Participatory and regional approach in forest planning. Present state and an ideal model for private land in Finland. *Reports of Finnish Environmental Institute* 26/2007, pp. 112–22.

9

Community forestry: a way forward

In developed regions, a recent interest in community forestry can be seen as a response to economic, environmental and social problems associated with conventional forest management. As described in the earlier chapters of this book, community forestry demands the broader integration of societal values and interests in forest governance. Consequently, its implementation in developed regions often requires restructuring the use and control of forest systems. Community forestry supporters see the approach as an opportunity to maintain local livelihoods, public access to open spaces and resources, and environmental conservation goals, as well as fairness and transparency in decision-making processes. Based on principles of local control, benefits and values, in theory community forestry offers an integrated approach to community development that is reinforced by parallel grassroots movements for participatory governance and civic environmentalism.

The stories in this book relay the bottom-up efforts of community groups, senior governments and forestry professionals (Chapters 3, 4, 5, 6) seeking an alternative to the status quo. Examining the history of community forestry in the eastern United States (Chapter 3) and Canada (Chapter 4) reveals that similar motivations were behind early community forestry programs and policies (i.e. concerns for remediation and conservation prompted by earlier poor land use practices) and that the two regions had a similar trajectory with respect to the rise and spread of municipal models (i.e. town and county forests). Community forestry experience in North America shows that, time after time, the community forestry concept has been revived during periods of heightened concern for ecological degradation, social conflict and

173

economic disaster – when it seemed all else had failed and a unique or innovative institutional response was needed.

It remains a challenge, however, for communities, governments and industry to collectively reframe community–forest relationships, in order to create space for local actors in forest governance (Bullock *et al.* 2012; Bullock, in press). Conceptualizing community forestry as governance (Chapter 7) means we must expand our views of conventional policy networks, and our understanding of how forest communities can be meaningfully involved in formerly closed forest management and planning processes. Under current arrangements on public land in Canada and the United States, an increasing variety of actors can become involved in defining and redefining forests: as economic base; as wilderness preserve; as traditional territory and homeland; as recreational playground. But linkages with the social domain imply that communities will also be defined and redefined: as labor source and service center; as scenic retreat and bedroom community; as decision-making and innovation hub.

Experiences in New England, coastal British Columbia and the American southwest (Chapter 3, 6 and 7) illustrate the kinds of contested landscapes that can provide the backdrop for community forestry. Emerging local control movements are typically catalyzed by environmental and economic crisis resulting from misuse of forest land and resources, and further driven by social conflict among grassroots actors and competing, often outside, development and environmental interests. In some settings, such as rural New England (Chapter 3) and coastal British Columbia (Chapter 6), former forest-based communities no longer solely depend upon timber extraction and wood processing. Economic restructuring in forestry and agriculture has decreased once-lucrative employment opportunities in many rural areas. In both North America and northern Europe, populations are becoming more urbanized. On the other hand, new individuals are streaming into rural regions to consume formerly productive landscapes as tourists and amenity migrants (see also Gill and Reed 1997). These residents and investors can bring new ideas and resources that further contribute to local economic, cultural and political transition.

It is important to view community forestry in terms of its relationship to the environmental and social conflicts that emanate from both state-led resource management and from local political processes. As discussed in the introductory chapter of this book, it may be that community forestry is not *the* answer, but that it is simply one option of many that could be used to achieve community goals and objectives.

Communities must come to understand *what* they think they want to do, but also *why*. Understanding how different groups construct rural communities, forests and community forestry, as well as the historical and geographical contexts of the place, is crucial to understanding local motivations. National surveys of community forest organizations and operations (e.g. Teitelbaum *et al*. 2006) and multiple case studies (e.g. Kusel and Adler 2003) indicate that diversity across locations and programs is the rule, not the exception. A wide variety of possible tenures, stakeholders and practices could be appropriate according to local conditions. For example, in instances where resource management and land-use planning has been historically top-down and centralized, and where economic systems have depleted resources, redirected benefit streams, and failed to generate wealth and to support communities, the motives for community forestry can be quite self-serving and exclusionary (such was the case in coastal British Columbia, as shown in Chapters 5 and 6). Community forests can privilege local residents over others, and they can be selective as to which interpretations of rural lifestyles are preserved (especially in cases involving private forest land where "outside" access and representation can be more easily obstructed) (Belsky 2008). Community forestry, whether a grassroots or provincially/state-imposed program, can induce conflict and be a centrifugal, rather than unifying, force.

However, in our view the presence of conflict, as a social phenomenon associated with community forestry, is not a simple case of "where there's smoke, there's fire." Conflict during the initial phases of community forestry is not unusual, nor does it point to some fundamental flaw in the concept or foreshadow the imminent failure of local organizing and decision-making efforts. Rather, conflict can be viewed as a symptom of grassroots democratic processes working through or transitioning between developmental stages. For example, the emergence of the Freedom Town Forest (Chapter 3), the Ontario Community Forest Pilot Program sites (Chapter 4), and all three community forest cases from British Columbia (Chapters 5 and 6) confirms previous research that characterizes stages in the development of new collaborative arrangements (Gray 1989; Selin and Chavez 1995; Plummer and FitzGibbon 2004). Researchers describe the emergence of community-based organizations through a self-organizing inter-organizational process that involves negotiating shared interpretations, information gathering and knowledge transfer, learning, increasing network linkages, and institutional structuring and formalization, as various actors adapt to and bring about change through their social interactions with the problem context. Collaborative community-based initiatives for community forestry (Sturtevant and Lange 2003), for co-management of river corridors, catchments, and estuaries (Olsson *et al.* 2004; Plummer 2006), and for UNESCO biosphere reserves (Ravindra 2004) demonstrate similar patterns, although they are not all exactly the same. The community forestry initiatives examined herein display a similar progression, "growing pains" and achievements.

Conflict over community forestry can indicate the existence of local frustrations with the nature or rate of change in a particular place, and hostile groups searching for a way to keep certain people "out" or maintain a fading way of life, which is of course an exercise in futility. Community forestry is not a way to halt change but instead offers a way for community members to learn about and understand what is changing in their forests and communities and why (and who is served by change versus the status quo). It provides a collaborative strategy to better adapt to and navigate unwelcome change in order to sustain forest communities based on the broadest range of local values and desires. Of course, in situations where polarization results from historic dislike among groups, entrenched beliefs and vested interests there is less hope for alignment. Communities engaged in local organizing and deliberative processes have an opportunity to collectively formulate shared understanding, values and experiences that form the basis of community identity. When motivated (or forced) to develop explicit goals and objectives for a community plan, community members engage in the refinement and improvement of decision-making processes and organizational routines needed for governance innovation, which is made possible through reflecting on misaligned perceptions, values and behaviors – otherwise known as *social learning* (Keen *et al.* 2005; Bullock *et al.* 2012). With proper support, and given the chance to resolve differences and issues, the outcomes of conflict are not always negative. The cases outlined in this book illustrate the potential benefits for communities in underdeveloped regions: increased local awareness, capacity, place-based information, political influence, trust and economic wealth are all examples of tangible outcomes.

ENGAGING COMMUNITIES IN FOREST GOVERNANCE
AND DEVELOPMENT

The previous chapters illustrate the historic resistance to the community forestry movement and the significant multi-scaled factors that have challenged its implementation. It is not surprising that community forestry has flourished when and where it has been backed by long-term state and provincial programs and resources, extension forestry, post-secondary institutions, service clubs and non-government organizations, and the media. As support for the community forestry concept presupposes awareness, promoting understanding of the concept and creating space for community forestry are joint concerns. For the most part, senior governments have been timid in the pursuit of community forestry policies, local advocacy has been largely reactive, and research has been unsystematic with pockets of albeit dedicated advocates and researchers working in relative isolation. There remains a lack of provincial/state vision, commitment and systematic approaches to implementing operational community forests, backed by well-developed policy and legislation, sectoral linkages, and integrated local and technical knowledge of social–ecological forest systems. But, as apparent in the cases presented in this book, these conditions are slowly changing.

For their part, the onus is on communities to develop the participatory capacity for local involvement in forest governance, to provide leadership and innovation in order to make the most of opening policy windows and opportunities, and to make forest management bureaucracies change. This is a serious void in some forest communities and regions where no community structures for resource management and development ever materialized, given the top-down tradition of provincial agencies and closed policy networks. However, proactive approaches to community-based monitoring and mapping, indigenous–municipal collaboration, and non-timber forest product development are just some initiatives that demonstrate the impact of community commitment.

Community groups do not necessarily need to "invent" new roles for themselves, but to promote their existing strengths and regain competencies that were once undertaken locally. The previous chapters in this book show that community forest organizations can develop and coordinate capacities that often get redirected to support dominant industries (e.g. as in Ontario, Chapter 4). The legacies of local planning exercises – social capital, technical expertise and information, and collective vision, for example – display the transferrable skills and assets that exist and that can be developed and harnessed to build community livelihoods. Opportunities exist to elevate the profile and application of community forest organizations in local and regional governance and administration, without downloading responsibilities from senior government or privatization. Where appropriate, community forest organizations could be engaged to address "governance gaps" in environmental resource and land management planning, economic development, and rural service delivery through involvement in, for example, fire interface work; pest control; food production; research and information generation; training and education; forestry consulting and extension work; and forestry contracting. Community forest forums also provide important public and political space to support civic participation and community organizing.

Developing an integrated knowledge base that is controlled by and accessible to the community is essential for effective local involvement in forest management. Possessing specialized information on the local setting improves local strategic and operational stance, and adds legitimacy to community forestry initiatives by bolstering resources. Information in the forms of maps and plans can provide universal tools and data display media to share and assert community desires and realities (Bullock *et al.* 2009). Local information (knowledge) also often already exists; it just needs to be organized into formats that can inform management. Local information generation can be a source of pride and symbol of progress, and give the community something to rally around. As illustrated in Creston (Chapter 5), field trips with community stakeholders aided knowledge transfer as well as increasing support for community forestry operations. The process of knowledge development and its outcomes can be a source of identity (trans)formation through which a "new" community emerges and political spaces are formed where decision-making can occur in new deliberative settings. Having specialized information to augment local and traditional knowledge for community forestry decision-making and organizing is critical to achieving integration as the basis of sustainable communities.

Beyond technical and operational considerations of community forestry, in North America and northern Europe growing and increasingly diverse populations call attention to the need to foster cross-cultural working relations and accommodate diverse local values (and regional values where community forests operate on public lands that provide significant ecosystem services) in forest governance. In particular, the need to respect indigenous rights and territorial claims cannot be overstated. Our case studies show that indigenous peoples, environmentalists and community forest managers are not automatic allies in community forestry. These groups can hold quite different values and interests, as well as levels of influence through various forums and policy networks. As illustrated in British Columbia (Chapters 5 and 6), some First Nations are very supportive of community forests but have other priorities and pressing issues to address, such as land claims, business ventures and social issues, which can make participation complex. In some instances, ecosystem-based planning has provided effective tools for regional economic and land-use planning. Ecosystem-based planning provides a framework that enables local values and needs to direct how institutions and operations will unfold. The holistic view achieved through ecosystem-based approaches is generally (and demonstrably) considered congruent with indigenous values and beliefs.

   In North America, various public–private–civic organizations, processes, legislative frameworks, ideologies and unforeseen events factor into a messy implementation setting. The cases examined in this book indicate just how difficult it can be to advance community forestry initiatives in the absence of suitable policies, sectoral support and/or well-developed local objectives. Reforming institutional frameworks, stakeholder power relations and, indeed, the structure and identities of communities is not a simple task. This does not mean, however, that it is impossible to alter existing socio-economic relationships, rules and practices (as dominant interests would sometimes have us believe). Whether in North America or northern Europe, shifting societal values and perceptions of forests are driving public demands for community forestry and local involvement in the decisions that affect the use and control of forest systems. Ongoing social change inevitably will influence human interactions with forest systems and how forestry is practiced (Kimmins 2002), as well as how forest-based development and forest community development evolve. The challenge then is envisioning what a well-developed governance system of networked community forests and sustainable communities should and will look like.

REFERENCES

Belsky, J. (2008). Creating community forests. In Donoghue, E. and Sturtevant, V. (eds.), *Forest Community Connections. Implications for Research, Management and Governance*. Washington, DC: Resources for the Future, 219–42.

Bullock, R. (in press). "Mill town" identity crisis: Reframing community and the culture of forest resource dependence in single industry towns. In Parkins, J. and Reed, M. (eds.), *Social Transformation in Rural Canada: New Insights into Community, Cultures, and Collective Action*. Vancouver, BC: UBC Press.

Bullock, R., Armitage, D. and Mitchell, B. (2012). Shadow networks, social learning, and collaborating through crisis: Building resilient forest-based communities in Northern Ontario, Canada. In Goldstein, B. (ed.), *Collaborative Resilience: Moving from Crisis to Opportunity*. The MIT Press, 309–37.

Bullock, R., Hanna, K. and Slocombe, S. (2009). Learning from community forestry experience: challenges and lessons from British Columbia. *Forestry Chronicle* **85**(2): 293–304.

Gill, A. and Reed, M. (1997). The reimaging of a Canadian resource town: post-productivism in a North American context. *Applied Geographic Studies* **1**(2): 129–47.

Gray, B. (1989). *Collaborating: Finding Common Ground for Multiparty Problems.* San Francisco, CA: Jossey-Bass.

Keen, M., Brown, V.A. and Dyball, R. (2005). *Social Learning in Environmental Management: Towards a Sustainable Future.* London, Sterling, VA: Earthscan.

Kimmins, J.P. (2002). Future shock in forestry: Where have we come from; where are we going; is there a "right way" to manage forests? Lessons from Thoreau, Leopold, Toffler, Botkin and Nature. *Forestry Chronicle* **78**(2): 263–71.

Kusel, J. and Adler, E. (eds.) (2003). *Forest Communities, Community Forests.* Lanham, MD: Rowman and Littlefield.

Olsson, P., Folke, C. and Hahn, T. (2004). Social-ecological transformation for ecosystem management: The development of adaptive co-management of a wetland landscape in southern Sweden. *Ecology and Society* **9**(4): 2.

Plummer, R. (2006). Sharing the management of a river corridor: A case study of the comanagement process. *Society and Natural Resources* **19**(8): 709–21.

Plummer, R. and FitzGibbon, J. (2004). Co-management of natural resources: A proposed framework. *Environmental Management* **33**(6): 876–85.

Ravindra, M. (2004). A road to tomorrow: Local organizing for a biosphere reserve. *Environments* **32**(3): 43–59.

Selin, S. and Chavez, D. (1995). Developing a collaborative model for environmental planning and management. *Environmental Management* **19**(2): 189–95.

Sturtevant, V. and Lange, J. (2003). From "them" to "us": The Applegate Partnership. In Kusel, J. and Adler, E. (eds.), *Forest Communities, Community Forests.* Lanham, MD: Rowman and Littlefield, pp. 117–33.

Teitelbaum, S., Beckley, T. and Nadeau, S. (2006). A national portrait of community forestry on public land in Canada. *Forestry Chronicle* **82**(3): 416–28.

Index

181